Best Easy Day Hikes Series

Best Easy Day Hikes
Syracuse

Randi Minetor

FALCONGUIDES

GUILFORD, CONNECTICUT
HELENA, MONTANA

AN IMPRINT OF GLOBE PEQUOT PRESS

Best Easy Day Hikes
Syracuse

Help Us Keep This Guide Up to Date

Every effort has been made by the author and editors to make this guide as accurate and useful as possible. However, many things can change after a guide is published—trails are rerouted, regulations change, facilities come under new management, etc.

We would love to hear from you concerning your experiences with this guide and how you feel it could be improved and kept up to date. While we may not be able to respond to all comments and suggestions, we'll take them to heart and we'll also make certain to share them with the author. Please send your comments and suggestions to the following address:

> Globe Pequot Press
> Reader Response/Editorial Department
> P.O. Box 480
> Guilford, CT 06437

Or you may e-mail us at:

> editorial@GlobePequot.com

Thanks for your input, and happy trails!

FALCONGUIDES®

Copyright © 2010 by Morris Book Publishing, LLC

FalconGuides is an imprint of Globe Pequot Press.

Falcon, FalconGuides, and Outfit Your Mind are registered trade-
marks of Morris Book Publishing, LLC.

TOPO! Explorer software and SuperQuad source maps courtesy of
National Geographic Maps. For information about TOPO! Explorer,
TOPO!, and Nat Geo Maps products, go to www.topo.com or www
.natgeomaps.com.

Maps by Off Route Inc. © Morris Book Publishing, LLC

Project editor: David Legere
Layout: Kevin Mak

Library of Congress Cataloging-in-Publication Data
Minetor, Randi.
  Best easy day hikes, Syracuse / Randi Minetor.
    p. cm. — (Falconguides)
  ISBN 978-0-7627-5465-6
  1. Hiking—New York—Syracuse—Guidebooks. 2. Trails—New York—
Syracuse—Guidebooks. 3. Syracuse (N.Y.)—Guidebooks. I. Title.
  GV199.42.N65M58 2010
  917.47'660444—dc22

                                                          2010005592
Printed in the United States of America

10 9 8 7 6 5 4 3 2 1

Contents

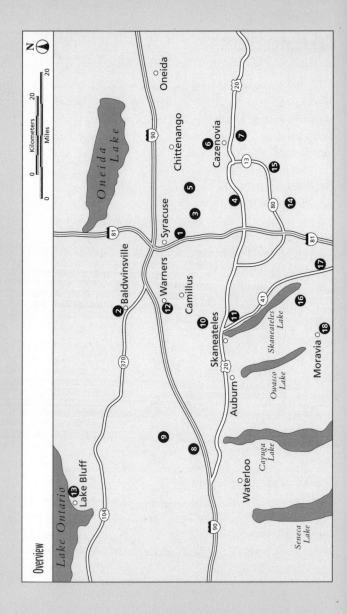

Acknowledgments

First and foremost, I am so grateful to my husband, Nic Minetor, for walking nearly all these trails with me, keeping me from getting hopelessly lost in the woods and knowing far better than I when it was time to stop hiking, stop writing, and see our friends again.

Thanks to Scott Adams, executive editor at Falcon-Guides, and everyone at Globe Pequot Press; they do such a careful and beautiful job in bringing our books to fruition. To my brilliant agent, Regina Ryan, I am undyingly grateful for all she does to manage the business of publishing on my behalf.

Kihm Winship, whom I have never met face to face, was uncommonly generous with his time and consideration in recommending a number of the trails that landed in this book (and thanks to Lorraine Woerner-MacGowan for suggesting I contact him). I am grateful to Tom Young and Pete Svitavsky at J. R. Clancy, Inc., in Syracuse for their recommendations and Margaret Potter at the Genesee Land Trust in Rochester for sending me to Stone Quarry Hill.

Several managers of beautiful natural spaces extended their assistance. My thanks go to Heidi Cortwright at Beaver Lake Nature Center, Joseph Scala at Stone Quarry Hill Art Park, Andrea Vanbeusichem at Montezuma National Wildlife Refuge, Jim Eckler at Howland Island, Gregory McGee and William Pavlus, who represent Skaneateles Conservation Area, Erin Agins and John Dimura of the New York State Canal Corporation, Diane Carlton at the New York State Department of Environmental Conservation, Abby Chermela at the Finger Lakes Land Trust, and Rick Banker at Fillmore Glen State Park.

I have so many friends to whom I am grateful, but Martin Winer, Ken Horowitz, and Rose-Anne Moore stand out from this group for their unflagging encouragement and support. In particular, Martin helped keep up the pace on a three-trail day that will live in infamy.

And finally, I thank all the clients of Minetor & Company, Inc., my public relations and corporate writing business, who put up with my days out of town and my erratic accessibility. Without you, none of these books could be possible. I cannot thank you enough.

Introduction

It's moments before dawn at the edge of a forested wetland surrounded by river and canal, as several small groups of people with binoculars in hand stand stock-still, listening intently.

There it is—the distant "Who cooks for you?" call of a barred owl, one of more than one hundred species that nest and breed in the refuge's forests. As darkness begins to recede and the light turns dawn-gray, a chirrup in the reeds on the edge of the forest signals a marsh wren's presence. A "witchity, witchity, witchity" song reveals a common yellowthroat's location, while deeper in the woods combinations of lyrical notes and lisping buzzes tell birders that black-throated green and black-throated blue warblers have arrived overnight.

With the brightening sky, more snatches of song fill the air. A rabbit crosses the now-visible path onto the island, and chipmunks begin their familiar sharp "chit" notes.

Where is this magical place? It's a few miles west of Syracuse at Howland Island, in the Northern Montezuma Wetlands Complex—one of many such refuges, forests, and preserves that provide homes to all manner of wildlife. Trails through this and more than a dozen other preserves present some of the most satisfying, easy hiking in the central New York region—all in places that allow us to connect with our natural world and all within an hour's drive of downtown Syracuse.

Take the Cliff Trail at Clark Reservation State Park or gaze beyond the cascading water at Chittenango Falls and see limestone and sandstone born as much as 400 million years ago, when a shallow sea covered much of North America. Clark Reservation's cliff edges rise high over the valley below, but they were not always so lofty. A diligently flowing creek created these tall places, wearing away at the stone banks until they became walls as the creek sank lower. Today we enjoy wide vistas and impressive rock formations because of millions of years of geology at work.

While limestone forms the bedrock of central New York, much of the landscape shows the effects of more-current events. Walk the ridgeline on the Esker Brook Trail in the Montezuma National Wildlife Refuge, circle the deep turquoise pools at Green Lakes State Park, or stroll the boardwalk to the kettle pond at Labrador Hollow Unique Area and see the impact of glaciers that moved over this land as recently as 20,000 years ago.

We know that receding glaciers hollowed out the crevasses that would become the Finger Lakes, but we may forget that the unusually deep ponds and small lakes are the products of huge blocks of ice that fell from calving glaciers, creating holes in the earth. When the ice blocks melted, they filled these holes with water and lakes were born. Today we can circle these unusual bodies of water on easy, level trails that reveal the lakes' unusual character.

There's at least one more chapter of natural history to discover in the Syracuse area: the twentieth century reforestation that's still in progress. We can enjoy easy or more rugged hikes through Baltimore Woods, Bear Swamp State Forest, and High Vista Nature Preserve because of the combined work of man and nature to reclaim this land.

Not so long ago—as recently as the 1930s—these properties were farmers' fields, used to graze cattle or grow crops. Today they are covered with young forests, planted in part by the legendary Civilian Conservation Corps of the Great Depression era. A delightful wilderness experience awaits visitors who explore each area on well-marked and maintained trails.

Intermixed with these excellent hiking experiences are some crown jewels within and just beyond Syracuse. Highland Forest County Park, with its meticulously labeled trails that traverse truly beautiful surroundings, offers one of the finest days out we've found anywhere. Fillmore Glen, the southernmost park in this guide, pairs an adventurous hike—aided by eight unobtrusive bridges—with a spectacular gorge, waterfalls, and startlingly emerald foliage.

Beaver Lake Nature Center, just north of the city in Baldwinsville, offers a series of delightful trails featuring an extended boardwalk along a tranquil lake. In the city, Elmwood Park stands as a triumph in natural landscaping, with its sets of stone steps and ramps that lead to shady, inviting woods. And the shores of Lake Ontario offer one of the area's most remarkable formations—Chimney Bluffs, where wind and weather combine to influence a towering, ever-changing coastline.

With so many options for day hikes, residents and visitors alike will find plenty of outdoor adventures that showcase the best of central New York—and all less than an hour's drive from the city of Syracuse.

Weather

Few places can match central New York for its gorgeous spring and summer, when flowers scent the air, leaves fairly burst from the trees in intense shades of green, and the sky turns cobalt to complement the sunlight.

The sun shines six days out of ten from June through August. Spring temperatures can linger in the 50s and 60s until June; idyllic summer days can average in the 70s and 80s, with occasional spikes into the 90s in June or July and cooler temperatures at night. Heavy rains often arrive in April, although they rarely last more than a day or two at a time. Syracuse has no dry season, so be prepared for rain any time you visit.

To truly appreciate this transformation to the Technicolor spring and summer seasons in upstate New York, however, we must face the Syracuse area's legendary winters. The city once rated fourth among the top-ten snowiest cities in America, and its heavy snowfalls continue to make national news.

Winter temperatures average in the mid-20s, with significant dips into the 20s, 10s, and single digits in January, February, and March. Check the windchill factor before making a winter hike, as the air can feel much colder than the temperature indicates. The annual February thaw can push temperatures into the 50s for a few days, but the cold will return, usually lasting into mid-April. Snow is guaranteed—an average winter sees 115 inches (that's 9 1/2 feet), although not all at once. In the winter months, November through January, the Syracuse area sees the sun about 28 percent of the time.

Fall equals spring in its spectacle, with days in the 50s and 60s, bright blue skies, and foliage panoramas throughout the area's parks and preserves.

Park and Preserve Regulations

You will find the lands listed in this book both accessible and fairly easy to navigate. Only the state parks listed charge admission fees (though some preserves suggest a donation).

While some of the parks have picnic areas with trash receptacles, most of the parks, forests, and preserves are "carry-in, carry-out" areas. This means that you must take all of your trash with you for disposal outside the park. Glass containers are not permitted in any of the parks.

Some preserves do not permit pets, and in all cases where they are allowed, dogs and other pets must be leashed. You will see dogs running free in some parks, but park regulations and county leash laws prohibit this. It's also illegal to leave your dog's droppings in the park; you can face fines for not cleaning up after your pet.

If you're a gun owner, you will need to leave your weapon at home when entering a county park, as only law enforcement officers are permitted to carry guns on these lands. Hunting is permitted in properties managed by the Department of Environmental Conservation, so it's a good idea to wear an orange jacket and hat if you're planning to hike these areas during hunting seasons.

Safety and Preparation

There is little to fear when hiking in upstate New York, whether you're stepping down into the gorge at Fillmore Glen or hiking through Bear Swamp State Forest. Some basic safety precautions and intelligent preparation will make your hikes calamity-free.

- **Wear proper footwear.** A pair of good, correctly fitting hiking shoes or boots can make all the difference on a daylong hike, or even on a short walk. Look for socks that wick away moisture, or add sock liners to your footwear system.

- **Carry a first-aid kit** to deal with blisters, cuts and scrapes, and insect bites and stings. Insects abound in late spring and summer in central New York, especially near wetlands, ponds, lakes, and creeks, so wear insect repellent and carry after-bite ointment or cream to apply to itchy spots.

- **Carry water.** Don't try drinking from the rivers, creeks, ponds, or other bodies of water unless you can filter or treat the water first. Your best bet is to carry your own—at least a quart per person for any hike and up to a gallon in hot weather.

- **Dress in layers,** no matter what the season. If you're a vigorous hiker, you'll want to peel off a layer or two even in the dead of winter. On a summer evening, the air can cool suddenly after sunset, and rain clouds can erupt with little preamble.

- **Bring your mobile phone.** All but the most remote trails in central New York have mobile coverage, so if you do get into a jam, help is a phone call away. (As a courtesy to the rest of us, set your phone to vibrate while you're on trail.)

- **Leave wildlife alone.** Central New York State once was home to the timber rattlesnake, but scientists believe this species to be extirpated from the areas covered in this book. Black bear sightings are very rare. As a general rule, don't approach wildlife of any kind. If you do see a bear, don't get any closer; if your presence changes its behavior, you're too close. Keep your distance and the bear will most likely do the same. Some cases of rabies in raccoons have been reported in the area; generally it's best to steer clear of these animals when they're seen in daylight.

Zero Impact

Many trails in the Syracuse area are heavily used year-round. As trail users and advocates, we must be especially vigilant to make sure our passage leaves no lasting mark. Here are some basic guidelines for preserving trails in the region:

- Pack out all your own trash, including biodegradable items like orange peels. You might also pack out garbage left by less considerate hikers.

- Don't approach or feed any wild creatures—the gray squirrel eyeing your snack food is best able to survive if it remains self-reliant. Feeding ducks and geese can spread illnesses among the birds when they come into contact while chasing bits of bread or corn. Please don't feed them.

- Don't pick wildflowers or gather rocks, antlers, feathers, and other treasures along the trail. Removing these items will only take away from the next hiker's experience.

- Avoid damaging trailside soils and plants by remaining on the established route. This is also a good rule of thumb for avoiding poison ivy and poison sumac, common regional trailside irritants.

- Be courteous by not making loud noises while hiking.

- Many of these trails are multiuse, which means you'll share them with other hikers, trail runners, cyclists, and horseback riders. Familiarize yourself with the proper trail etiquette, yielding the trail when appropriate.

- Use restrooms or outhouses at trailheads or along the trail.

Land Management Agencies

These government and nonprofit organizations manage most of the public lands described in this guide. They can provide further information on these hikes and other trails in the greater Syracuse area.

- City of Syracuse Department of Parks, Recreation & Youth Programs, 412 Spencer St., Syracuse 13204; (315) 473-4330; www.syracuse.ny.us/parks
- New York State Canal System, 200 Southern Blvd., Albany 12201; (800) 4CANAL4 (422-6254); www.nyscanals.gov
- New York State Department of Environmental Conservation, Region 7 Office, 615 Erie Blvd. West, Syracuse 13204; (315) 426-7400; www.dec.ny.gov
- Onondaga County Parks & Recreation, 106 Lake Dr., Liverpool 13088; (315) 451-7275; onondagacounty parks.com/
- New York State Office of Parks, Recreation and Historic Preservation, Empire State Plaza, Agency Building 1, Albany 12238; (518) 474-0456; nysparks.state.ny.us

How to Use This Guide

This guide is designed to be simple and easy to use. Each hike is described with a map and summary information that delivers the trail's vital statistics including length, difficulty, fees and permits, park hours, canine compatibility, and trail contacts. Directions to the trailhead are also provided, along with a general description of what you'll see along the way. A detailed route finder (Miles and Directions) sets forth mileages between significant landmarks along the trail.

Hike Selection

This guide describes trails that are accessible to every hiker, whether visiting from out of town or living in the greater Syracuse area. The hikes are no longer than 8 miles round-trip, and some are considerably shorter. They range in difficulty from flat excursions perfect for a family outing to more challenging treks along the area's gorges and ravines. While these trails are among the best, keep in mind that nearby trails, often in the same park or preserve, may offer options better suited to your needs.

I've sought to space hikes throughout the Onondaga, Cayuga, Madison, Cortland, and Wayne County areas. Wherever your starting point, you'll find a great easy day hike nearby.

Difficulty Ratings

These are all easy hikes, but easy is a relative term. Some would argue that no hike involving any kind of climbing is easy, but in the Syracuse area hills and ravines are a fact of life. To aid in the selection of a hike that suits particular needs and abilities, each is rated easy, moderate, or more challenging. Bear in mind that even more challenging routes can be made easy by hiking within your limits and taking rests when you need them.

- **Easy** hikes are generally short and flat, taking no longer than an hour to complete.

- **Moderate** hikes involve increased distance and relatively mild changes in elevation; they will take one to two hours to complete.

- **More challenging** hikes feature some steep stretches and/or greater distances; they generally will take longer than two hours to complete.

These are completely subjective ratings—consider that what you think is easy is entirely dependent on your level of fitness and the adequacy of your gear (primarily shoes). If you are hiking with a group, you should select a hike with a rating that's appropriate for the least fit and prepared in your party.

Approximate hiking times are based on the assumption that on flat ground, most walkers average 2 miles per hour. Adjust that rate by the steepness of the terrain and your level of fitness (subtract time if you're an aerobic animal; add time if you're hiking with kids) and you have a ballpark hiking duration. Be sure to add more time if you plan to picnic or take part in other activities like bird watching or photography.

Trail Finder

Best Hikes for Birders

2   Beaver Lake Nature Center: Lake Loop Trail
8   Montezuma National Wildlife Refuge: Esker Brook Trail
9   Northern Montezuma WMA: Howland Island
14 Labrador Hollow State Unique Area
15 Highland Forest County Park
17 High Vista Preserve

Best Hikes for Waterfalls

4   Pratt's Falls Park
6   Chittenango Falls State Park
11 Skaneateles Conservation Area
18 Fillmore Glen State Park

Best Hikes for Water Views

2   Beaver Lake Nature Center: Lake Loop Trail
3   Clark Reservation State Park
5   Green Lakes State Park
9   Northern Montezuma WMA: Howland Island
12 Erie Canalway Trail: Warners to Camillus
13 Chimney Bluffs State Park
14 Labrador Hollow State Unique Area

Best Hikes for Fall Foliage

Best Hikes for Panoramic Views

Map Legend

	Interstate Highway
	U.S. Highway
	State Highway
	Local Road
	Unpaved Road
	Featured Trail
	Trail
	River/Creek
	Body of Water
	Boardwalk/Steps
	Bridge
	Camping
	Information Center
	Parking
	Picnic Area
	Point of Interest/Structure
	Restroom
	Town
	Trailhead
	Viewpoint/Overlook

1 Elmwood Park: Upper Tree Trail

This urban getaway's well-developed trails and remarkably diverse forest provide a sense of wilderness in the midst of the bustling city.

Distance: 1.0-mile loop
Approximate hiking time: 40 minutes
Difficulty: Easy
Trail surface: Packed dirt trail, stone stairs
Best season: Apr through Nov
Other trail users: Dog walkers, joggers, cross-country runners
Canine compatibility: Leashed dogs permitted
Fees and permits: No fees or permits required

Schedule: Open daily, dawn to dusk
Maps: National Geographic Topo!, New York/New Jersey edition
Water availability: Restrooms in park
Trail contact: City of Syracuse Department of Parks, Recreation & Youth Programs, 412 Spencer St., Syracuse 13204; (315) 473-4330; www.syracuse.ny.us/parks

Finding the trailhead: Glenwood Avenue, Elmwood Avenue, Fairfield Avenue, and Craddock Street form the park's boundaries in the city of Syracuse. From NY 173 (West Seneca Turnpike), take NY 80 North 1.2 miles to Elmwood Avenue. Turn left onto Elmwood and then take a right onto Clyde Avenue. The park entrance is on the left. Drive in and park in the parking lot at the end of the road. The trail begins from the parking lot. GPS: N43 01.137' / W76 10.002'

The Hike

Since its inception as a park in 1927, Elmwood Park has attracted a steady daily stream of people from the surrounding neighborhood who walk their dogs, jog the trails, look for nesting birds, play on Little League teams, and enjoy many other activities in this urban haven.

The park, a glacially sculpted valley with a quietly flowing creek called Furnace Brook, manages to harbor more than fifty species of conifer and hardwood trees on its thickly forested slopes. The Upper Tree Trail, a set of developed pathways through this remarkable woodland, brings walkers the pleasures of this cool, shaded grove and its wealth of flowering shrubs and small, furry animal life.

Walk up the slope from the parking area or take one of the rough stone staircases to the trail and you'll soon reach a plateau from which you can look down into the forest's hidden gully. In spring last year's leaves delicately cover the gully's slopes, but in fall brilliant colors blanket the ground as the surrounding oaks, maples, cherries, and many other trees scatter their jewel tones over the forest floor. You may choose to walk down into the gully itself—a gentle slope down and a gradual incline back to the trail—or follow the trails along the top, as our directions suggest.

As you walk here, look for sugar maple, northern white cedar (what some call arborvitae), yellow birch, bitternut hickory, and northern red oak trees, among many others. Wildflowers can be abundant here, and wide patches of vinca (periwinkle) bloom in early spring, covering some areas with purple blossoms. Watch for red and gray squirrels, chipmunks, eastern cottontails, and woodchucks; add raccoons and opossums to your list if you walk here in early evening or toward dusk.

Spring birds here include an abundance of warblers, from yellow to black-throated blue, as well as hermit and wood thrushes, rose-breasted grosbeaks, robins, blue jays,

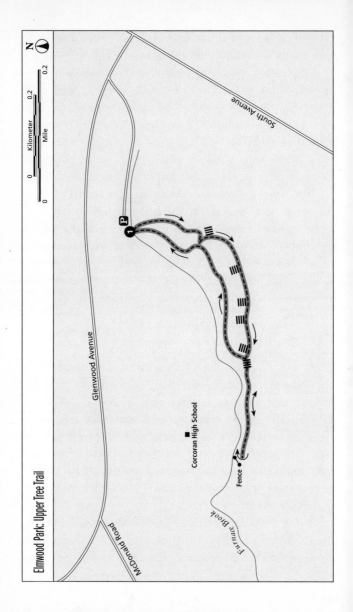

Elmwood Park: Upper Tree Trail

cardinals, and several sparrow species. Red-eyed vireos sing daily here in spring, and orioles are a common sighting.

If you enjoy your walk here, thank the Elmwood Park Neighbors Association for their diligent work in keeping this park clean and advocating for its maintenance.

Miles and Directions

0.0 Start at the parking lot; walk up the road and past the barrier at the end. Continue straight on the paved path up the hill. Turn left into the woods, and walk uphill on the dirt path.

0.2 Reach the first of several sets of steps on your left, which lead up into the neighborhood that flanks the park. Pass these and continue on the path. In about 300 feet the trail forks right and left. Go left.

0.3 The trail goes right, left, and down the steps straight ahead. Take the path to the left. In about 200 feet, steps go down to the right of the path. Continue straight.

0.4 The trail goes straight as well as down to the right ahead. Continue straight. Bear left at the next intersection and begin the trail through the park's extension.

0.6 The spur trail ends at a fence with an opening to your right for access to Corcoran High School. There's parking here and a bridge across Furnace Brook. The trail to the left goes up to the school's athletic fields. Turn around here and retrace your steps up the spur trail.

0.7 Stairs here go down to the bridge over Furnace Brook. You came here on the trail to your right; now take the trail on the left along the ridge.

0.9 Reach an intersection of two trails; continue straight (bearing right).

1.0 Walk down the slope or take the stairs to the parking area, as you prefer.

2 Beaver Lake Nature Center: Lake Loop Trail

Wander the perimeter of Beaver Lake through meadows, woods, and bog for a generous sampling of all the earthly delights this nature center offers.

Distance: 3.0-mile loop

Approximate hiking time: 1.25 hours

Difficulty: Easy

Trail surface: Packed dirt trail and boardwalk

Best season: Apr through Nov

Other trail users: Joggers, cross-country skiers

Canine compatibility: Dogs not permitted

Fees and permits: Entrance fee per vehicle, paid as you exit; annual pass available

Schedule: Open daily, 7:30 a.m. to dusk; closed Thanksgiving and Christmas

Maps: Onondaga County Parks; available online at www.onon dagacountyparks.com/beaver

Water availability: At the visitor center

Trail contact: Beaver Lake Nature Center, 8477 East Mud Lake Rd., Baldwinsville 13027; (315) 638-2519; www.onondaga countyparks.com/beaver

Finding the trailhead: From Syracuse on I-690 North, exit at West Genesee Street (NY 370). Turn west (left) and drive 1.8 miles to East Mud Lake Road. Turn right onto East Mud Lake and continue to the nature center entrance at 8477 East Mud Lake Road, on the left. The trail begins at the parking lot. GPS: N43 10.809' / W76 24.137'

The Hike

One of the Syracuse area's most satisfying hiking experiences awaits you at Beaver Lake, where the nature center provides enough habitat diversity to attract more than 200 bird species, hundreds of plant species, and all of central New York's most common mammals.

A 200-acre lake forms the centerpiece of this natural space, while hardwood forest, open meadows, and a wetland bog surround the lake. The Lake Loop hike traverses all of these habitats, bringing you closer to songbirds and waterfowl, squirrels and chipmunks, and a landscape that changes with the seasons, offering you wide views in winter and early spring and protecting nesting species in spring and summer.

The carefully maintained trail leads to a lengthy boardwalk through the reeds and willows on the lake's north side, where you can explore the marshland without wading through mud and muck. Watch here for red-winged blackbirds that scold as they try to draw your attention away from the reedy areas—they almost certainly have nests nearby. A muskrat may swim past with only a nose above the water, and Canada geese arrive by the thousand in the fall to rest and feed before heading to warmer climates.

As you come into the home stretch on the Lake Loop Trail, a short connecting path leads to the Three Meadows Trail. You may wish to detour and enjoy this loop, which winds through wildflower-rich open land loaded with grassland birds like savannah and song sparrows, blackbirds, eastern meadowlarks, and occasional bobolinks. Watch for northern harriers swooping over the field as they pursue their supper and for short-eared owls hunting at dusk in the winter months.

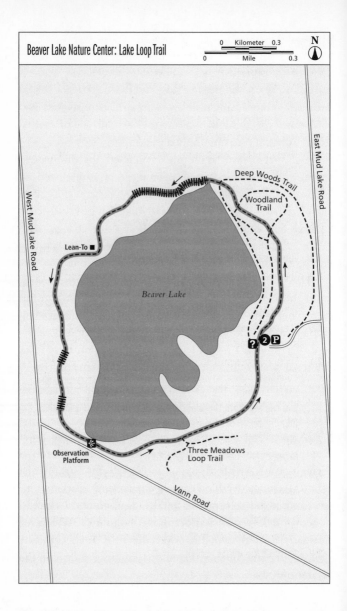

Beaver Lake Nature Center: Lake Loop Trail

0 — Kilometer — 0.3
0 — Mile — 0.3

N

West Mud Lake Road

East Mud Lake Road

Deep Woods Trail

Woodland Trail

Lean-To ■

Beaver Lake

? 2 P

Observation Platform

Three Meadows Loop Trail

Vann Road

Miles and Directions

0.0 Start by walking across the lot to the Lake Loop trailhead. If you are facing the visitor center, the well-marked trailhead is to your right.

0.2 An unmarked trail goes off to the left. Continue straight.

0.3 The Woodland Trail crosses here. Continue straight.

0.4 The Woodland Trail crosses the Lake Loop again. Keep going straight.

0.6 The Deep Woods Trail crosses the loop. Stay straight on the Lake Loop.

0.7 The boardwalk through the wetland begins.

0.8 This is a great spot for a wide view of Beaver Lake.

1.1 The boardwalk ends and the packed dirt trail resumes.

1.3 The trail to the right goes to a log hut—a lean-to used in nature center programs. Continue straight.

1.7 Reach another boardwalk, shorter than the first.

1.8 The boardwalk ends. Reach another short boardwalk in about 300 feet.

2.1 There's an observation platform to your right, at a level with Vann Road. You can see an unofficial but well-worn trail up to the platform. The expansive water view to your left is what you will see from the platform. About 300 feet ahead, the trail crosses a service road. Continue straight.

2.4 Reach the connecting trail to the Three Meadows Trail loop to your right. Continue straight.

2.9 You've nearly reached the parking area. Turn left; the Three Meadows trailhead is to your right. The parking lot is visible ahead and to the right. To the left is the visitor center, where the trail officially ends. Walk the last 500 feet to the visitor center (which has a great gift shop) to complete the loop.

3.0 Arrive at the visitor center.

3 Clark Reservation State Park

Choose an easy amble through a quiet wood or a more rugged hike along a limestone outcropping above a deep, glacially carved lake.

Distance: 2.2-mile loop
Approximate hiking time: 1.25 hours
Difficulty: More challenging
Trail surface: Packed dirt trail, limestone rock
Best season: Apr through Nov
Other trail users: None
Canine compatibility: Leashed dogs are permitted
Fees and permits: Entrance fee per vehicle on weekends and holidays from Memorial Day to Labor Day; annual pass available
Schedule: Open daily, dawn to dusk; trails closed in winter
Maps: Available at park entrance station
Water availability: Drinking fountain outside the nature center
Trail contact: Clark Reservation State Park, 6105 East Seneca Turnpike, Jamesville 13078; (315) 492-1590; nysparks.state .ny.us/parks/info.asp?parkID=17

Finding the trailhead: From Syracuse take I-481 South to the Jamesville exit (exit 2). Turn left and take Jamesville Road south 1.3 miles to NY 173. Turn right onto NY 173 and continue 1.25 miles to the park entrance. The trail begins at the nature center, just off the parking area. GPS: N42 59.700' / W76 05.652'

The Hike

Named a "reservation" because the government set the land aside for Revolutionary War veterans back in 1792, this dramatically beautiful state park never passed to the heroes of that time—none of them claimed their share—but it managed to escape lasting development before it became parkland in 1926. Today we can enjoy the extraordinary scene created by glaciers some 10,000 to 20,000 years ago, laced with hints of the shallow sea that covered most of the continent hundreds of millions of years earlier.

Glacier Lake, one of the park's most significant land-marks, is a glacial plunge pool—a deep bowl carved by torrents of meltwater as glaciers of the last ice age receded from this area. The lake is 62 feet deep, and its surface water does not mix with its bottom water, making this one of only a handful of meromictic lakes in the United States. The result is an astonishing clarity that allows visitors to see what lies below the surface in remarkable detail.

Your hike can be an easy walk along the Mildred Faust Trail or a more challenging trek along the Lake Trail to the Cliff Trail, with a 330-foot change in elevation in a brief 0.2-mile incline. The Faust Trail leads through woodland in which you may see any number of the 300 fern and flowering plant species documented here, as well as more than eighty tree and shrub varieties. Wildflowers abound here in spring and summer, and trees come into bloom in mid-May, filling the air with their fragrances.

The Lake Trail, a flat but rugged hike, follows the northern shore of Glacier Lake over rocks and fallen trees along a dirt path. The trail climbs quickly to the Cliff Trail, from which you can enjoy a spacious view of the thick forest across the water and the deeply turquoise lake below. You'll traverse a series of limestone slabs along the cliff's edge and climb several short stone stairways to reach the highest point on the trail (at about 740 feet). From here the trail becomes easy again as you follow the Faust Trail into the woods and back to the parking area.

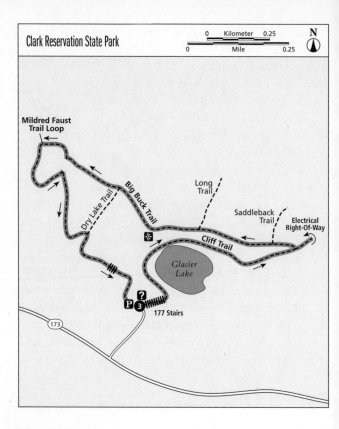

Miles and Directions

0.0 Start at the nature center and take the stairs down to the Lake Trail (177 steps in all). At the bottom of the stairs, turn left onto the Lake Trail.

0.1 Follow the Lake Trail along Glacier Lake. The trail is rocky but fairly level and well blazed with green paint on the trees. (These are the only distinct blazes you will find in the park.) The path provides terrific views of the lake—look at the edges, where you can see entire trees that have fallen into the water as the earth eroded under their roots.

0.7 Reach the top of the only major incline on this part of the trail. Continuing straight will take you to a power line right-of-way that stands at the edge of the park; if you've reached the power lines, you've gone too far. Turn around to your left and follow the Cliff Trail. In about 450 feet the Saddle Back Trail goes to your right. Continue straight.

0.9 Take the steps up to the limestone ledge. Look left for great views of the lake and the distant forest. The path is wide, but there's no railing here; take care as you walk.

1.0 The Long Trail goes off to the right. Continue straight.

1.2 Reach the last great overlook point before you leave the Cliff Trail. Take time to enjoy the view before turning right onto the Big Buck Trail.

1.4 The Big Buck Trail intersects the Dry Lake Trail. Continue straight.

1.5 Turn right onto the Mildred Faust Trail loop.

1.8 Turn right to begin the return route on the Faust Trail.

2.0 The trail turns sharply left, then right. Pass the Dry Lake Trail junction to your left and continue on the Faust Trail. In about 450 feet the Table Rock Trail goes left. Continue straight.

2.1 Cross a boardwalk.

2.2 Turn right and continue to the parking area, which you will reach in about 350 feet.

4 Pratt's Falls Park

A quick descent to a rushing cascade followed by an easy walk through a cool woods make this a great little hike for families with children.

Distance: 0.9-mile loop

Approximate hiking time: 30 minutes

Difficulty: Easy, with some stairs

Trail surface: Packed dirt trail, rock stairs

Best season: Apr and May, Sept and Oct

Other trail users: None

Canine compatibility: Leashed dogs permitted

Fees and permits: Donation per vehicle

Schedule: Apr through Oct, 8:30 a.m. to sunset; Nov through Mar, 10:00 a.m. to 4:00 p.m.

Maps: Park map available online at www.onondagacountyparks .com/pratts

Water availability: Restrooms in parking area in season or at the park office

Trail contact: Pratt's Falls Park, 7671 Pratt's Falls Rd., Manlius 13138; (315) 682-5934; www .onondagacountyparks.com/pratts

Finding the trailhead: From US 20 in Pompey take Henneberry Road north 2 miles to CR 218 (Pratt's Falls Road). Turn right onto CR 218 and continue to the park entrance. The trail begins at the parking area. GPS: N42 55.899' / W75 59.589'

The Hike

If you're heading into the forested country south of Syracuse for a picnic or a grand day out, Pratt's Falls is a must-see stop: This park features a 137-foot ribbon cascade falls with a viewing platform that brings you close enough to feel the freshwater spray when the waterfall is at its fullest in spring.

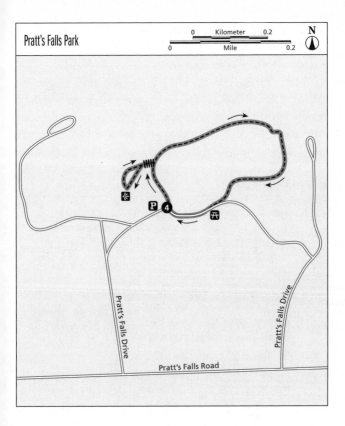

Pratt's Falls served area residents well in the days before European settlers' arrival, providing a plentiful water supply and fishing for the Seneca Indians who made their home in and around this park. Later the falls became the site of the first mill in Onondaga County, providing power for a sawmill as early as 1796 and later a gristmill as well.

The brief walk down the steps to the waterfall only whets visitors' appetites for more of the park, so consider this short hike once you've ascended the stairs, especially if you have children who will enjoy a little more time in the woods before or after your picnic.

The trail leads along the Limestone Creek gorge and through hardwood forest, then away from the creek as it arcs farther into the woods. In a few minutes the trail emerges at the edge of a picnic area, looping back along the edge of the woods to the parking area.

Miles and Directions

0.0   Start at the parking area and look for the gateway sign that says FALLS TRAIL. Pass under this sign to the stairs and descend to the first level. Turn left to proceed down the ramp to the stairs that lead to the falls (seventy-seven stairs in all).

0.2   At the bottom of the stairs, the Falls Overlook provides the best head-on view of Pratt's Falls. On sunny days, watch for rainbows in the spray above the cascading waters. Return up the stairs to the junction with the rest of the trail.

0.3   Go straight to continue the trail loop.

0.7   The trail follows a level path through the forest, emerging here at the edge of the picnic area. Turn left or right to continue along the woods' edge to your picnic table or to the parking area.

0.9   Complete the loop by returning to the parking lot and your vehicle.

5 Green Lakes State Park

Two deep, turquoise lakes, an old-growth forest, and a veritable festival of wildflowers and wildlife combine to make this one of the most popular easy hikes in the Syracuse area.

Distance: 3.1-mile loop
Approximate hiking time: 1.5 hours
Difficulty: Easy
Trail surface: Packed dirt trail, some paved sections
Best season: Apr through Nov
Other trail users: Joggers, cross-country skiers, cyclists
Canine compatibility: Leashed dogs permitted

Fees and permits: Entry fee per vehicle
Schedule: Open daily, dawn to dusk
Maps: Available at park entrance
Water availability: Restrooms in parking area or at clubhouse
Trail contact: Green Lakes State Park, 7900 Green Lakes Rd., Fayetteville 13066; (315) 637-6111; nysparks.state.ny.us/parks/info.asp?parkID=23

Finding the trailhead: From Syracuse take I-690 East 7 miles to NY 290 East. Continue on NY 290 for 10 miles to the park entrance at Green Lakes Road. After the ticket booth, park in the area near Green Lake Beach. GPS: N43 03.489' / W75 57.879'

The Hike

Few central New York hikes pack as much fascinating geology, beautiful scenery, and accessible wildlife watching into one walk as does Green Lakes State Park—so it's no wonder that this park attracts visitors from all over the area to circle its lakes on foot, on skis, or by bicycle. As lovely as it is geologically significant, Green Lakes offers an easy walk with enough length and variation to hold a hiker's interest over and over again.

The two lakes—sometimes a bright turquoise, sometimes emerald green—credit their vibrant color to a combination of factors. Thousands of years ago, a massive waterfall created by glacial meltwater pounded this area, sculpting the deep lakes you see here and a handful of others, including Glacier Lake in Clark Reservation State Park. This forceful formation caused the lakes to become meromictic. While most lakes experience a turnover of their waters with the temperature changes of spring and fall, pulling silts from the lower waters up to the surface, Green and Round Lakes do not turn over. The result is the eerie clarity you see here—with objects well below the surface standing out in sharp relief—and the resulting light penetration produces the saturated shades of emerald and cyan.

This hike takes you around both lakes, crossing between them along a merry stream that connects their waters. As you leave Green Lake and begin your circuit of Round Lake, stop to admire Round Lake's color and its idyllic setting. In 1973 this 170-foot-deep lake was designated a National Natural Landmark by the National Park Service as one of only a few meromictic lakes of this depth in the United States. The adjacent one hundred acres of old-growth forest contains trees that are hundreds of years old. You can explore this area further on the Old Growth Trail, a loop that leads away from Round Lake from the lake's southwest side.

Such an exciting landscape naturally attracts all manner of wildlife, from the ubiquitous chipmunks to white-tailed deer, as well as migrating warblers, wood thrush, woodpeckers (including the magnificent pileated woodpecker), cedar waxwing, and many others.

As you come into the last leg of this trail, don't miss Deadman's Point, an actual reef—like you'd find under the ocean—created by a buildup of a calcium carbonate substance called marl. Bacteria produce the marl on an ongoing basis, expanding the reef as it encrusts algae, mosses, and even fallen trees. This striking sight makes for a weirdly pretty underwaterscape on the edge of Green Lake.

Miles and Directions

0.0 Start at the Green Lake Beach parking area. The trail begins as a paved path.

0.2 The pavement ends and the trail surface becomes crushed stone and a groomed dirt path.

0.4 Pass a set of wooden stairs going up the hill to your right. Continue straight.

0.8 Take the cross trail to your left to continue to Round Lake. This little trail takes you past the stream that connects the two lakes.

0.9 Cross the bridge over the connecting stream and turn right.

1.0 The path to the right goes to a platform overlooking the stream. Stop here before continuing to Round Lake. You'll reach the lake in about 300 feet. A marker here explains Round Lake's National Natural Landmark status.

1.4 Reach a bridge over a low spot that affords a terrific view of the lake through the trees. You can see entire trees that have collapsed into the lake here. In a few feet you'll come to the junction with the Old Growth Trail. If you'd like to take this short loop trail, turn left. Otherwise continue on the Round Lake Trail. As you come around the western side of the lake, the park's high hills rise on your left. Watch the understory for ground-feeding thrushes and sparrows.

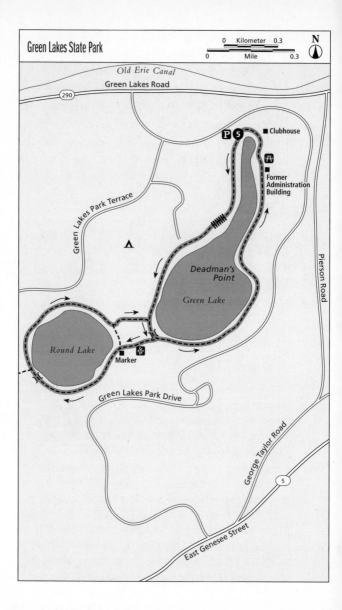

Green Lakes State Park

0 Kilometer 0.3
0 Mile 0.3

N

Old Erie Canal
Green Lakes Road
290

P 5 ■ Clubhouse

Green Lakes Park Terrace

■ Former Administration Building

Deadman's Point

Green Lake

Pierson Road

Round Lake

■ Marker

Green Lakes Park Drive

George Taylor Road

5

East Genesee Street

1.9 The trail goes straight and to the left. To complete the figure eight, turn left onto the connector trail.

2.0 Turn right to complete the loop around the east side of Green Lake. Continue straight on this trail around the lake.

2.5 You've reached Deadman's Point, which is easy to see at any time but is at its most vivid when lake levels are lower in summer and fall. When you're ready, continue on the trail around the lake.

2.7 A trail to the right leads to a picnic area. Continue straight. The large building ahead to the right is the former administration building, constructed in the 1930s by the Civilian Conservation Corps.

2.9 The trail reaches the paved pathway around the clubhouse and the beach. Continue on the paved path to the parking area.

3.1 Arrive back at the parking area.

6 Chittenango Falls State Park

Descend into a gorge for head-on views of a 167-foot waterfall, then meander through woods and meadows filled with fruit trees and flowering shrubs.

Distance: 2.2-mile loop
Approximate hiking time: 1.25 hours
Difficulty: Easy
Trail surface: Packed dirt trail, some paved sections, stone and wooden stairs
Best season: Apr through Nov
Other trail users: Cross-country skiers
Canine compatibility: Leashed dogs permitted
Fees and permits: Entrance fee in season

Schedule: Open daily, dawn to dusk
Maps: Park map available online at NYFalls.com and www.nyfalls.com/downloads/maps/chittenango-park-map.pdf
Water availability: Restrooms on second level
Trail contact: Chittenango Falls State Park, 2300 Rathbun Rd., Cazenovia 13035; (315) 655-9620; www.nysparks.com/parks/info.asp?parkId=11

Finding the trailhead: From Syracuse take I-481 south to exit 3E toward Fayetteville. Turn right onto East Genesee Street/NY 5 and follow NY 5 east for 10.4 miles to Route 13 South. Turn right on NY 13 South and travel 6 miles to the park entrance, which will be on your right. The trail begins at the parking lot. GPS: N42 58.696' / W75 50.577'

The Hike

Note: The Gorge Trail is only open from late spring to late fall.

Begin at the top of one of central New York's hidden gems, where Chittenango Falls tumbles an impressive 167 feet over a series of ridges in the north-flowing Chittenango Creek. Whether it's a leisurely trickle in the heat of summer or a rushing torrent in early May, this waterfall reveals more than 400 million years of geologic history behind its descending waters.

Many eons ago, when a shallow sea covered the land that would become North America, limestone and dolomite rocks formed as silt, sand, and other sediments drifted with the water to the sea's floor. You can see the layers of these early rock formations in the stratified sedimentary wall behind the falls. Observant hikers may find fossils in the rocks along the creek and throughout the park, the remnants of aquatic creatures that made their home in that primordial sea.

In addition to all that remains from prehistoric times, Chittenango Falls State Park provides a breeding ground for contemporary animals and plants as well. The Chittenango ovate amber snail—a tiny critter less than an inch long that lives on the slopes alongside the waterfall—lives only in this park and nowhere else in the world. Fewer than twenty-five of these snails existed as recently as 1990.

See if you can spot roseroot, an endangered flowering plant that lives here in the park and in only two other places in New York State. It clings to high, sheer ledges in the gorge near the falls along with Hart's-tongue fern, which loves rocky environments with consistent moisture. Bring binoculars to get a good look at both of these plants in spring and summer.

Your hike takes you down into the gorge for magnificent head-on views of the falls and the roiling creek at its base, so bring your camera: By the time you reach the bottom of the stone and wooden staircases that lead into the gorge, you'll stand on a pedestrian bridge that places the falls front and center for your photographic enjoyment. Then it's back up the steps to explore a section of the park that receives less attention but provides a solid hike through forest, meadows, and hedgerows of wild flowering shrubs.

Miles and Directions

0.0 Start at the parking lot. Walk to the paved footpath and turn right to reach the overlook at the top of the falls. When you're ready to continue, you'll see the path to the lower overlook points on your right. Start down the stairs.

0.1 Reach the middle overlook, with your first head-on view of the falls. Continue down the stairs to the pedestrian bridge.

0.2 Walk out on the pedestrian bridge for the best view of the falls yet. If the Gorge Trail is open, you can cross the bridge and return to the top of the gorge using this trail. If it isn't, go back up the stairs the way you came.

0.4 You are back at the top of the stairs. Take the paved path and continue until you see the sign for the Charcoal Chips Trail (the C trail on the park's map) in about 250 feet. Turn right onto this trail, cross the bridge over the wash, and continue straight as you follow the yellow trail markers.

0.7 Turn right at this intersection. Continue to follow the yellow trail markers.

0.8 The trail goes two ways here: straight and up to the left. Go straight across the bridge over a stream. You'll cross another bridge shortly, and then the trail splits. Go straight up the hill.

0.9 Several trails meet here. You'll see green trail markers here for the park's Meadow Trail—the "D" trail on the map displays in the park. Follow these to the left.

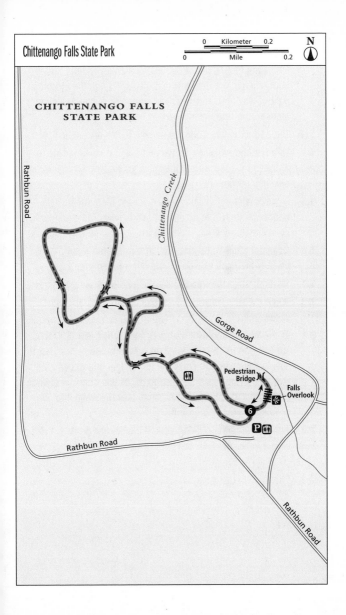

CHITTENANGO FALLS
STATE PARK

Rathbun Road

Chittenango Creek

Gorge Road

Pedestrian
Bridge

Falls
Overlook

6

Rathbun Road

Rathbun Road

0   Kilometer   0.2
0   Mile   0.2

N

1.0   Take the trail to the right over the bridge. From here follow the bright-orange plastic trail markers you'll see on sticks, indicating trail "E". In about 250 feet cross another bridge, then emerge in a meadow that also serves as the electrical right-of-way for the local power company. A steady incline leads to the next intersection.

1.3   The trail turns left. Continue straight to the next intersection.

1.4   Turn left and cross the bridge and begin a steep incline to an open meadow. In the meadow, go straight through the next intersection.

1.5   Follow the green plastic markers for the Meadow Trail (the park's "D" trail). The orange trail ends here. The green trail goes straight and left. Take the left.

1.6   Continue straight, up and around through the swamp grass, up over the knoll and down into the wooded area.

1.7   Travel through the wooded area, carefully crossing the creek.

1.8   When the trail reaches a T, turn right and link back with the yellow trail.

2.1   At the intersection with the road, keep left. About 250 feet straight ahead, the trail leads to private property. Turn left to stay in the park, and cross the footbridge. In another 150 feet turn left to reach the restrooms, or turn right to continue to the parking lot. Cross the bridge over the wash into the developed area of the park.

2.2   Arrive back at the parking lot and the starting point of the trail.

7 Stone Quarry Hill Art Park

Art meets nature among the meadows, hedgerows and woodlands of this quirky space, each made greater by sweeping views of the countryside.

Distance: 1.5-mile loop
Approximate hiking time: 45 minutes
Difficulty: Easy
Trail surface: Packed dirt, mowed grass, some crushed gravel
Best season: Apr through Nov
Other trail users: Cross-country skiers, snowshoers
Canine compatibility: Leashed dogs permitted
Fees and permits: Donation suggested
Schedule: Open daily, dawn to dusk
Maps: Park map available online at www.stonequarryhillartpark .org/
Water availability: On the hilltop near the Studio Gift Shop
Trail contact: Stone Quarry Hill Art Park, 3883 Stone Quarry Rd., PO Box 251, Cazenovia 13035; (315) 655-3196; www .stonequarryhillartpark.org

Finding the trailhead: From Syracuse take I-690 East to I-481 South to exit 3E toward Fayetteville. Follow NY 92 for 12.7 miles to US 20. Turn left onto US 20 and follow it to Stone Quarry Road; turn right. Pass the buildings and park in the gravel lot at the top of the hill. Begin the hike at the Vista trailhead. GPS: N42 54.668' / W75 50.056'

The Hike

This quirky little 104-acre park hosts a variety of outdoor art, created and installed by emerging and established artists from all over the country. Exhibitions feature new works every year, many of which you will discover as you walk the easy, rolling trails. Come in the summer and view work in any number of media, from recycled materials to cast concrete, each appearing in the woods or on the hilltop. Even the trees and shrubs become part of the art using intriguing labels, a particularly appropriate cluster of trunks, or an appealing setting to turn the natural into the intentional.

The hike travels through alternating meadows, tight woodlands, and formerly tilled fields, establishing a patchwork of outdoor spaces in regular sequence. Begin on the Vista Trail with the panoramic view that gives the trail its name—a vast green and gold countryside in New York's Finger Lakes region.

Your hike follows the Woodland Trail, the Secret Garden Trail (which oddly does not actually feature a garden), and the Hawthorn and Old Quarry Trails, climaxing in an equally compelling viewpoint to the north. The final leg swings up between the meadow's edge and the Hedgerow, finally rejoining the Secret Garden Trail and ending at the Vista once again.

To extend your park experience, pick up a nature brochure at the hilltop kiosk or, on weekends, in the Studio Gift Shop (open Friday through Sunday, noon to 5:00 p.m. during the exhibition season), and explore the other 3 miles of trails.

As in many other small parks, trails crisscross one another and beg to lead you astray at nearly every intersection. If you keep the hilltop as your North Star, you will find your way back even if you wander onto one of the outer trails (Watershed or Meadow View).

Most important, be sure to make the turn off the Link Trail (blue markers)—part of the venerable Finger Lakes Trail and a connecting path for the North Country National Scenic Trail. The North Country Trail begins in eastern upstate New York and continues all the way to North Dakota, covering 625 miles in New York State alone and more than 2,000 miles along its full length. While you may yearn to tackle a long-distance trail, that's probably not why you've come to Stone Quarry Hill—so make the turn onto the Secret Garden Trail at the 0.3-mile point.

Miles and Directions

0.0 Start on the gravel path that begins at the southern end of the parking lot. You'll see a sign for the Vista Trail. As you walk from here, the wide-angle view of New York's southern tier comes into view.

0.1 Enter the woods. Note the double blue markers on a tree at the edge of the woods. The Link Trail is the blue trail; follow this for now. In about 250 feet a trail goes off to the left. Continue straight.

0.2 Follow the orange marker for the Woodland Trail to the left. Soon you will see a blue marker for the Link Trail, going to the right. Turn right. (The Woodland Trail continues straight.)

0.3 Turn left at the meadow. In about 250 feet enter the woods and begin the Secret Garden Trail. Follow the blue marker to the left at the next intersection, then go straight and follow the Secret Garden loop. In a few steps, a narrow wooden plank system covers a wet spot. Continue straight.

0.4 At the pavilion in the clearing, turn left and pick up the path at the woods. You'll pass a pond on the way. The next intersection comes up quickly; turn left at the OLD QUARRY TRAIL sign and follow the white markers. Soon you'll emerge in a

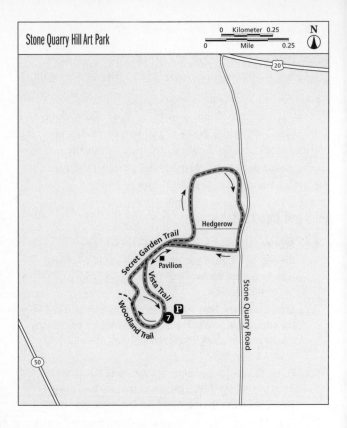

0   Kilometer 0.25
0   Mile   0.25

N

Hedgerow

Secret Garden Trail

Pavilion

Vista Trail

Woodland Trail

Stone Quarry Road

7 P

50

20

meadow—continue straight and reenter the woods. Then turn right onto the Hawthorn Trail.

0.7 At the intersection with the Watershed Trail, turn right and return to the meadow. Turn left onto the meadow edge and follow the mowed path. From here the trail begins a series of steady but gradual inclines, rising to a great view of Cazenovia Lake to the southwest and the hilly terrain to the south.

1.0 The Old Quarry Trail goes right; continue straight through the hedgerow and along another meadow. Turn right at the woods and continue along the hedgerow.

1.2 Reach a parking lot and gravel path to the road on your left. (Option: For a shortcut back to your car, turn left and walk along the road.) Continue straight to pick up the Secret Garden Trail again. In about 450 feet you'll reenter the woods on the Secret Garden Trail.

1.3 Turn left and walk straight across the meadow on the mowed path, up the last incline before the parking lot.

1.4 Turn left at the gravel path and walk around the rest of the Vista Trail for some northern views before returning to your vehicle.

1.5 Arrive back at the parking lot.

8 Montezuma National Wildlife Refuge: Esker Brook Trail

This quiet ramble follows a glacially created ridge through a hardwood forest that echoes with birdsong, ending at a tranquil wetland pond.

Distance: Three trails; any two yield a 1.3-mile loop
Approximate hiking time: 40 minutes
Difficulty: Easy
Trail surface: Dirt path
Best season: Apr through June, Sept through Nov
Other trail users: Birders
Canine compatibility: Leashed dogs permitted
Fees and permits: No fees or permits required
Schedule: Open daily, dawn to dusk. All Esker Brook Trails and South Spring Pool Trail close during white-tailed deer hunting season (Nov 1–mid-Dec)

Maps: Refuge maps available online at www.fws.gov/r5mnwr/refuge_map.html
Water availability: At the visitor center; open Apr 1 through Oct 31, 10:00 a.m. to 3:00 p.m. weekdays, until 4:00 p.m. weekends; weekends only in Nov; closed Dec through Mar
Trail contact: Montezuma National Wildlife Refuge, 3395 US 20 East, Seneca Falls 13148; (315) 568-5987; www.fws.gov/r5mnwr
Special considerations: Insect repellent a must from May through mid-Sept

Finding the trailhead: Take the New York Thruway (I-90) west to exit 40 (Weedsport). Turn right at NY 34 and right again at NY 31. Continue 10.6 miles and turn left onto NY 89 (Armitage Road). Drive about 1.5 miles and turn left onto Wiley Road (continue to follow NY 89). Pass the Tschache Pool parking area, cross over the Thruway, and turn right onto East Tyre Road. Continue to the Esker Brook Trail parking area and trailhead. GPS: N42 58.452' / W76 47.030'

The Hike

Three trails follow this edge of Montezuma National Wildlife Refuge, a protected wetland since 1938 and one of the most popular landing grounds in upstate New York for tens of thousands of Canada and snow geese, ducks, gulls, and terns every spring and fall. Esker Brook Trail skirts the western edge of the refuge, which offers shelter and plentiful feeding to migrating songbirds throughout the months of May, September, and October.

Your walk follows the Ridge Trail into a forest of leafy hardwoods with a dense understory of berry-bearing shrubs, which produce their brilliant fruit in late summer and fall. Ferns, broadleaf groundcover, and wildflowers effectively obscure the forest floor from late April until the leaves fall in early November.

From this excellent vantage point, you may find yourself eye to eye with a thrilling variety of warblers in spring—black-and-white, Blackburnian, black-throated blue and green, Nashville, chestnut-sided, bay-breasted, magnolia, Canada, Wilson's, Tennessee, and even occasional Connecticut warblers light here on their way to parts north in May or south in September. Vireos, thrushes, and sparrows can be thick in these woods during the migration and mating seasons, and you are certain to encounter tight flocks of ruby-crowned kinglets in early May, probably fraternizing with black-capped chickadees and tufted titmice.

The Ridge Trail then reveals the neighboring countryside, crossing the edge of an open field filled with wildflowers in spring and summer and alive with bird activity. The trail terminates as it reaches two ponds, favorite places for swimming muskrats as well as belted kingfishers, green and great blue herons, and wood ducks. As you circle the ponds in the second segment of your walk, watch along the edges of the reeds for common moorhens and elusive Virginia rails. Spring peepers will fill the air with their song on warm days in April, and hawks—including the ospreys and bald eagles that nest in the refuge—may pass overhead.

When you've returned almost to your starting point after your pond loop, take the Orchard or Brook Trail back through the woods. You'll be closer to the forest floor on this trail, following the brook at the bottom of the esker. Here you have a better view of the wildflowers and other plant life that form the area's ample understory, making this the best place to watch for ground-feeding birds like thrushes and white-crowned and white-throated sparrows, as well as eastern cottontails, chipmunks, gray squirrels, and raccoons at dawn and dusk.

Miles and Directions

0.0 Start at the trailhead in the parking lot. Enter the woods at the Ridge trailhead, at the west end of the lot. Cross a bridge over Esker Brook. As you enter the woods, the trail will take you to the left through the forest. The trail gives you an opportunity to look down into the forest to your right, a great way to look for treetop-dwelling warblers, vireos, woodpeckers, jays, and other migrants.

0.1 The South Spring Trail goes right here, leading through a wetland and out to NY 89. Enjoy the wide view of the countryside as you continue straight on the Ridge Trail.

0.5 The Pond Trail goes right; the Brook Trail goes left. Turn right. This part of the path is mowed grass and can be very wet

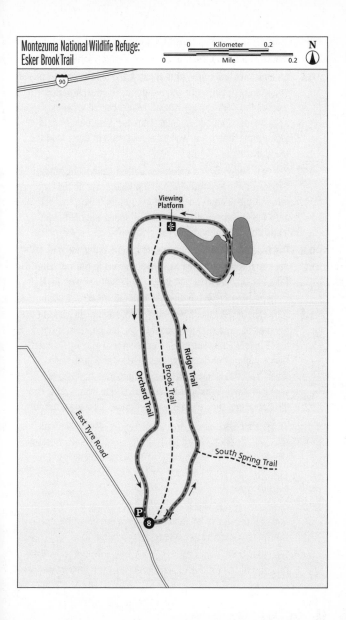

Montezuma National Wildlife Refuge:
Esker Brook Trail

0   Kilometer   0.2

0   Mile   0.2

N

90

Viewing
Platform

Ridge Trail

Orchard Trail

Brook Trail

East Tyre Road

South Spring Trail

P
8

in spring or after heavy rain. Watch for belted kingfishers, marsh wrens, and swamp sparrows as you circle the pond.

0.6 An indistinct trail to the right through the shrubs offers an opportunity to circle the second pond. The easier route crosses the dike straight ahead, with excellent viewing of both ponds. Continue straight. Look for great blue herons—a Montezuma staple—as well as elusive rails or bitterns in the tall grasses.

0.7 Reach a bridge over a brook—actually a connecting stream between the two ponds. After the bridge, trails go right (around the second pond) and left (return trails). Turn left onto the Orchard Trail. In about 300 feet a set of steps leads down to a pond-viewing platform.

0.8 The Brook and Orchard Trails split here. Each leads directly back to the parking area at different levels in the woods. Take the Orchard Trail and watch for ground-feeding birds, chipmunks, squirrels, and frogs hopping across the path.

1.3 Turn right at the intersection and proceed straight ahead to the parking area. Before you leave the refuge, drive around the 3-mile Wildlife Drive loop, especially in May or October. Concentrations of ducks, grebes, geese, and gulls here reach National Geographic–style proportions during the spring and fall migration. When a peregrine falcon drifts over the flocks and they all take wing at once, it's a sight not to be missed.

9 Northern Montezuma WMA: Howland Island

With its wide trails, alternating meadows and shady woodlands, and a network of ponds that attract thousands of migrating waterfowl, Howland Island is a wilderness paradise.

Distance: 5.7-mile lollipop
Approximate hiking time: 2.5 hours
Difficulty: Moderate due to length
Trail surface: Dirt and gravel roads
Best season: Apr through Nov
Other trail users: Cross-country skiers, cyclists, horseback riders
Canine compatibility: Leashed dogs permitted
Fees and permits: No fees or permits required

Schedule: Open daily, dawn to dusk
Maps: Available at Montezuma Audubon Center, SR 89, Savannah, 13146; (315) 365-3580
Water availability: None
Trail contact: NYSDEC, Northern Montezuma Field Office, 1385 Morgan Road, Savannah 13146, (315) 365-2134; also friendsof montezuma.org
Special considerations: In summer wear a hat, sunscreen, and insect repellent.

Finding the trailhead: From Syracuse take the New York Thruway (I-90) west to exit 40. Follow NY 31 West and turn right onto NY 89. Continue on NY 89 to Savannah-Spring Lake Road and turn right. Follow Savannah-Spring Lake Road to Carncross Road. Turn left onto Carncross and continue until the road dead-ends at Howland Island. Park here and cross the bridge into the wildlife management area. GPS: N43 04.700' / W76 42.242'

The Hike

The Seneca River and the Erie Canal surround this 3,500-acre island, sequestering this patch of leafy woodlands, managed ponds, and open meadows and contributing to its preservation. Under the watchful management of the New York State Department of Conservation and a host of dedicated volunteers, this jewel in central New York's tiara provides one of the most appealing hiking experiences in the area—for those who are willing to take on some distance to reach its most compelling sections.

You'll walk a mile just to reach the first major intersection in the maintenance road network, but from here the marshes spread before you with their wealth of plant and animal life and their abundant bird populations. In late spring and throughout the summer, waterfowl can be hard to find. But in the fall, when leaves turn amber and cinnamon, the skies fill with V formations of Canada and snow geese, and migrating ducks arrive with the first gusts of north wind. By mid-September migrating warblers and vireos descend on the island in fallouts by the hundred, while thrushes flit through by night, their chip notes the only evidence of their stealthy passage.

Beyond its status as a birders' paradise, Howland Island serves up a colorful helping of spring and summer wildflowers and fall berries. Dame's rocket line the roads with their nodding clusters of petals, while daylilies spring from gatherings of slender, dark green leaves on the roadside. Daisy fleabane, trillium, chicory, and Shasta daisy are just a few of the blooming varieties found here.

The second-growth forests provide long stretches of delightful shade, alternating with the meadows and cultivated fields and edging the open ponds. Managed to provide habitat for migrating waterfowl and rare marsh birds, these ponds also furnish a breeding ground for turtles, many frog species, and those banes of every hiker's existence: mosquitoes and deer flies. Be sure to apply plenty of insect repellent before venturing into Howland Island, especially in the heat of summer. You may want to choose a cooler spring or fall day for this hike, as the bugs can be fierce when the air is humid.

Miles and Directions

0.0 Start from the parking area and walk past the yellow gate to the long, straight trail ahead. The trail is a dirt road through grassland dotted with small, excavated vernal ponds, alternating with stands of deciduous trees. An agricultural field opens out past the woods.

0.7 A dirt road goes right, into the field. This access road heads south to Hickory Hill. Continue straight.

1.0 A dirt road crosses here to the right and left. There's a storage building on the hill to your left. Continue straight; you'll come out on this road later, on the return route.

1.2 A road goes left here. You can see a marshy pond (Brooder Pond) ahead to the left. Continue straight down the dike between Brooder and Headquarters Ponds.

1.6 The road forks to the left and right just past Winter Pond. Take the road to the left. You'll have a nice view of CCC Pond just around the corner.

1.9 The path crosses a dike between Goose Pond on the right and Breeder Pond on the left. After the dike, Arum Pond appears on your right as you climb the hill to a meadow of tall grasses.

2.3 After a wooded section, Black Duck Pond appears on the left. You can still see Arum Pond on the right. Another

access road goes right here; stay on the main trail and continue to your left around Black Duck Pond.

2.6 Turn left. Cook Pond is ahead on your right.

2.8 At Cook Pond the path goes straight and to the left. Continue straight.

3.5 A faint path goes right. Turn left. You are now on the road you crossed earlier, back at the 1.0-mile point.

4.7 Turn right at the intersection to head back to the parking area.

5.7 Arrive back at the entrance and parking area.

10 Baltimore Woods Nature Center: Boundary Trail

Circle this charming woodland on a trail through open meadows filled with wildflowers and a cool forest alive with birds and chipmunks.

Distance: 2.7-mile loop
Approximate hiking time: 1.25 hours
Difficulty: Moderate
Trail surface: Dirt path
Best season: Apr through Nov
Other trail users: None
Canine compatibility: Dogs not permitted
Fees and permits: No fees or permits required; donations encouraged

Schedule: Open daily, dawn to dusk
Maps: Trail map available online at www.baltimorewoods.org/AboutUs/Hikingtrails/
Water availability: At visitor center
Trail contact: Baltimore Woods Nature Center, 4007 Bishop Hill Rd., Marcellus 13108; (315) 673-1350; www.baltimorewoods.org

Finding the trailhead: From Syracuse take I-81 South to I-481 North and continue to exit 1 (Rock Cut Road/Brighton Avenue). At the light turn left onto NY 173 (West Seneca Turnpike). Continue 2.6 miles to NY 175 West. Pass through the town of Marcellus, and turn left onto South Street. At the Y in the road, bear right onto Bishop Hill Road. Park in the lower parking area for Baltimore Woods. GPS: N42 57.943' / W76 20.633'

The Hike

This natural restoration of a former working farmland spans more than 180 acres with woods that feature hemlock as well as central New York's more typical maple, oak, tulip tree, beech, and northern white cedar. The center is not named for its previous owner, however: The story goes that the farmer decided to break with the local tradition of marketing his cattle in New York City, choosing to farm in this location because of its proximity to the railroad line to Baltimore. So well known was he for this departure that people referred to his land as "Baltimore" . . . and the name stuck.

The loop trail around this mature hardwood forest introduces you to Baltimore Woods with a sampling of the nature center's scope, passing through forest and open field, down into the valley and across a creek, and out to the farmers' fields that flank the center's borders.

Spring and summer are excellent times to walk these woods, when red-eyed vireo and eastern peewee call in alternating shifts and downy, hairy, and pileated woodpeckers rattle the trees with their drumming. Chipmunks dig their burrows right into the trail, popping their heads out and diving back in as your footsteps warn them of your arrival. Red and gray squirrels are a certain sighting, and there's a distinct possibility of spotting raccoon, fox, or deer, especially toward sunset.

Wildflowers fill the open fields with blue phlox, dame's rocket, Queen Anne's lace, and daisies, while mayapple blooms in the woods' understory and trillium pokes out from the leaf cover. Watch for wild strawberry in the grassy areas, and see if you can beat the birds and small animals to the berries in June.

Miles and Directions

0.0 Start from the parking area and take the Valley Trail (yellow plastic markers on the trees) to the Boundary Trail. Walk in

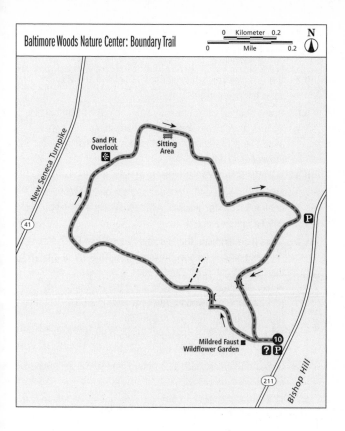

at the trailhead to the first post, and continue straight ahead
onto the Valley Trail.

0.1 Reach the Mildred Faust Wildflower Garden, a cultivated
garden that can help you identify flowers that are in bloom.
Continue straight.

0.3 Turn right at the trail junction.

0.4 Cross the bridge over the creek. In a moment you'll reach the intersection with the Boundary Trail. Turn left, following the pink markers.

0.5 The Overlook Trail goes right here. Continue straight and cross the creek again.

0.6 Reach another creek crossing. From here the trail gradually inclines as you come out of the woods into a more open area. Plenty of wildflowers find footing here. You'll reenter the woods in a bit.

0.9 The nature center's boundary is to the left; a farmer's plowed field reaches beyond. Continue straight on the path and enter a field of tall grasses. As the trail bends right, you'll enter a former orchard.

1.1 Cross the road here, then ascend to the Sand Pit Overlook. The sand pit can be seen to your right—it's more of a ridge than a pit, from which sand erodes with wind and weather. Proceed through an open field along the park boundary and back into the woods. You'll walk along a ridge, with the brook babbling below you to the left.

1.4 As you descend from the ridge toward the forest floor, there's a sitting area with two benches overlooking the brook. You may want to stop here before you begin the next ascent from the valley.

1.7 At the trail intersection turn right. (The trail to the left goes to Phillips Pond.)

1.9 Reach an intersection with the Field and Forest Trail. Turn left.

2.0 After a walk along the forest floor, cross into an open meadow where dandelions dominate in spring. Pass another mowed path to the left and continue straight.

2.2 Come to a tricky intersection, just before you reach the center's other parking lot (not the one where you parked earlier). Turn right and follow the Field and Forest Trail (green markers).

2.3 At the next intersection continue straight and follow the gray arrows to the visitor center.

2.4 Turn left at this intersection with the Griffiths and Valley Trails. You're now following a section of the Valley Trail that you did not hike earlier. Remember to follow the yellow markers now.

2.6 Cross a bridge over the brook and begin your final ascent out of the valley to the parking lot. Turn left at the power line right-of-way and continue to the parking area.

2.7 Arrive back at the visitor center and your vehicle.

11   Skaneateles Conservation Area

Take a brisk, short walk along a creek to a shimmering cascade, followed by a wander in a peaceful wood.

Distance: 1.0-mile loop
Approximate hiking time: 30 minutes
Difficulty: Easy
Trail surface: Dirt path
Best season: Apr through Nov
Other trail users: Trail runners
Canine compatibility: Leashed dogs permitted
Fees and permits: No fees or permits required
Schedule: Open daily, dawn to dusk
Maps: National Geographic Topo!, New York/New Jersey edition
Water availability: None
Trail contact: Town of Skaneateles, 24 Jordan St., Skaneateles 13152; (315) 685-3473; www.townofskaneateles.com
Special considerations: Wear bright orange clothing during the hunting season—May, Nov, and Dec.

Finding the trailhead: From Syracuse take NY 5 West 10.6 miles to NY 321 South. Continue to the intersection of Old Seneca Turnpike (just past Welch-Allyn). Turn left onto Old Seneca. The second road on the right is Gully Road; turn right. The parking lot is on the right in about a mile. GPS: N42 58.085' / W76 23.409'

The Hike

Named for English dairy farmer William Guppy, Guppy Falls is the main attraction at this little preserve. The 23-foot-high waterfall descends over a ridge in the Skaneateles Formation, a shale and sandstone bedrock compression that dates back to the Devonian period in the world's geologic history—some 390 to 415 million years ago.

This hike takes you to a point near the top of the falls

where you can view the cascading waters from above before winding through the fairly young forest. Climb the stairs at the southeast corner of the parking area and follow the Rudl Trail—named for Tim Rudl, the Eagle Scout who participated in its construction—about 0.25 mile to the falls overlook (at 840 feet). After the falls overlook, the trail winds through the woods, providing an opportunity to see how a forest can regenerate on cleared farmland once the plows and cows leave the land behind.

During late April and early May, wildflowers abound along the ravine to the left of the trail: Look for white and red trillium, trout lily, Solomon's seal, false Solomon's seal, red and white baneberry, bloodroot, blue cohosh, perfoliate bellwort, wild leek, hepatica, and foam flower. To your right, however, the land is devoid of wildflowers; so far, flowering plants have not spread naturally into the old cultivated areas. Watch for two sections peppered with red flags, which mark permanent plots where naturalists have planted native forest wildflowers in an effort to restore native vegetation to the regenerated, post-agricultural forests. You are welcome to investigate these experimental areas, as long as you leave the plot markers in place.

Miles and Directions

0.0   Start at the parking area, following the sign that says WALKING TRAIL. Following the yellow markers, begin by climbing fifty-nine steps and crossing a small bridge.

0.3   The orange trail goes right here. Continue straight along the ridge to the Guppy Falls overlook.

0.5   The white trail turns right here. Continue to follow the yellow markers.

0.7   The yellow trail turns right, while the red trail continues

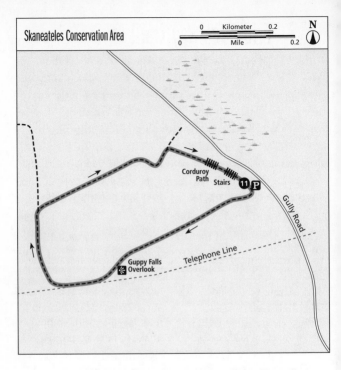

Skaneateles Conservation Area

Corduroy Path
Stairs
11 P
Gully Road
Telephone Line
Guppy Falls Overlook

ahead. Turn right, following the yellow markers. The trail narrows and becomes a slender path through the woods, sometimes becoming indistinct in the thick understory.

0.8 In wet seasons there's a small stream here. You should be able to step over it or cross on rocks and logs in higher water. In a moment, the yellow trail joins the blue trail and turns left.

0.9 Turn right on the yellow path (red goes straight here). Cross a stream on the partial bridge or on rocks. A corduroy section of the path begins ahead (logs laid down side by side over a wet area). At the end of the corduroy, you've completed the loop; take the stairs down to the parking area.

1.0 Arrive back at the parking area.

12 Erie Canalway Trail: Warners to Camillus

This straight, shaded, 2.0-mile trail segment reaches the mid-point of the original Erie Canal at Sims' Store.

Distance: 4.2 miles out-and-back or 2.1-mile shuttle

Approximate hiking time: 1.5 hours for out-and-back hike. 1 hour or less for shuttle

Difficulty: Easy

Trail surface: Stone dust, section of dirt road

Best season: Year-round

Other trail users: Joggers, cyclists, cross-country skiers, snowmobilers in one section

Canine compatibility: Leashed dogs permitted

Fees and permits: No fees or permits required

Schedule: Open daily, dawn to dusk

Maps: Trail map available online at www.nyscanals.gov

Trail contact: New York State Canal System, 200 Southern Blvd., Albany 12201; (800) 4CANAL4 (422-6254); www.nyscanals.gov

Finding the trailhead: From Syracuse take NY 173 West 9.8 miles to Warners. Erie Canal Park in Warners is at the corner of Newport Road and NY 173 (Warners Road). Park in the parking area off Newport Road. For a shuttle hike, leave a vehicle at Erie Canal Park in Camillus, 5750 Devoe Rd.; (315) 488-3409. GPS: N43 03.162' / W76 18.237'

The Hike

From Albany to Buffalo, the Erie Canal towpath provides some of the most pleasant walking, biking, skating, and running trail footage in New York State, with about 380 miles of level, meticulously maintained pathways. This tiny segment of the total trail extends through Erie Canal Park northwest of Syracuse, ending in Camillus at the exact midpoint of the original canal and the 300-acre Erie Canal Park.

This sample packs a great deal of canal history into its 2.0-mile stretch. A trace of the original Erie Canal, this was one of many sites that experienced significant improvements during the period of the Enlargement, from 1836 to 1862. Working to accommodate more and heavier barges—early barges weighed perhaps 30 tons, while boats carrying cargo in the early 1900s often weighed in at 3,000 tons—the Enlargement increased the canal's width from 40 to 70 feet, with a new depth of 7 feet instead of the 4 feet of water that had buoyed the lighter barges.

You'll actually walk on the towpath used by mules and oxen that towed barges along the canal, led by a "hoggee"— a boat driver, most often a boy in his teens. Today this canal segment is lined on either side by verdant foliage, with shade trees providing a sense of seclusion along the man-made waterway. The flat, easy walk ends at Camillus Erie Canal Park, where volunteers maintain a set of reproductions of buildings that stood here at the canal's halfway point in the 1800s. Plan to spend some time in the Sims' Store Museum, a carefully reproduced canal-side store circa 1860s that supplied merchants and barge drivers with medicines, food, water, and animal feed. (Check the museum's current hours at www.townofcamillus.com.)

If you enjoy this short hike, consider a longer trek along the canal. The Old Erie Canal State Historic Park maintains 36 miles of the original canal and its modern trail from DeWitt to Rome, east of Syracuse, where hikers are joined

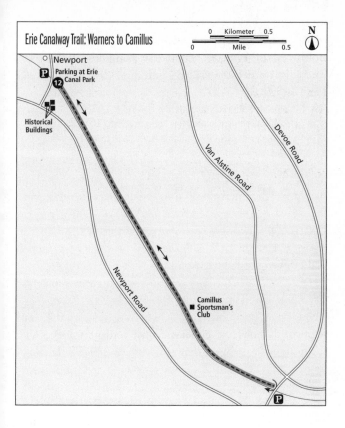

Erie Canalway Trail: Warners to Camillus

0   Kilometer   0.5

0   Mile   0.5

N

Newport

Parking at Erie
Canal Park

12

Historical
Buildings

Van Alstine Road

Devoe Road

Newport Road

Camillus
Sportsman's
Club

by paddlers, kayakers, horseback riders, and snowmobilers
for year-round outdoor recreation.

Miles and Directions

0.0 Start the hike on the stone-dust path along the canal. (FYI:
There's a paved path into the park here; be sure to take the
towpath on the edge of the canal.)

1.4 The trail becomes a shared road, with limited vehicular traffic. The road provides access only to the Camillus Sportsman's Club, so very few cars pass through here. The speed limit is 10 miles per hour.

2.1 Reach Erie Canal Park in Camillus; the historic building reproductions are on your left. The canal path continues from here to Lockport, New York, northeast of Buffalo. If you haven't arranged for a shuttle, turn back toward Warners and retrace your steps on the canal path.

4.2 Arrive back in Warners. From here the canal path continues to Waterford, New York, east of Albany.

13 Chimney Bluffs State Park

Hike through an evergreen forest and along a high bluff to see the effects of wind, storm and winter on this Great Lake ridgeline.

Distance: 2.2-mile loop

Approximate hiking time: 1 hour

Difficulty: Moderate

Trail surface: Dirt path

Best season: June through Sept

Other trail users: None

Canine compatibility: Leashed dogs permitted

Fees and permits: Entry fee in season

Schedule: Open daily, dawn to dusk

Maps: Park map available online

at nysparks.state.ny.us/parks/info.asp?parkID=168

Water availability: Restrooms at parking lot

Trail contact: Chimney Bluffs State Park, 7700 Garner Rd., Wolcott 14590; (315) 947-5205; nysparks.state.ny.us/parks/info.asp?parkID=168

Special considerations: Bluff Trail is on the edge of a high bluff with no railings. This hike is not recommended for young children.

Finding the trailhead: From North Syracuse take I-481 North 20.3 miles to NY 3 West. Continue on NY 3 West 8.3 miles and turn left onto NY 104 West. Take NY 104 West 14.2 miles to County Road 163 and turn right. Continue on 163 2.5 miles to County Road 143 (Ridge Road) in Wolcott, and turn right. Turn right again on County Road 150, and continue north to Slaght Road. Turn left and drive on Slaght to East Bay Road, and turn right. Continue 0.2 mile to the park entrance on Garner Road. The trail starts on a paved path from the parking lot. GPS: N43 16.871' / W76 55.345'

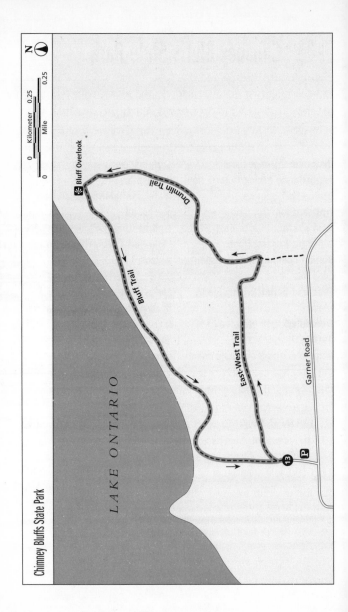

Chimney Bluffs State Park

LAKE ONTARIO

Bluff Overlook

Bluff Trail

Drumlin Trail

East-West Trail

Garner Road

13
P

N

0   0.25
Kilometer

0   0.25
Mile

The Hike

If you doubt the greatness of the Great Lakes, Chimney Bluffs is the place for a change of mind and heart. Here Lake Ontario matches its big brother, Lake Superior, in magnificent scenery sculpted by the sheer force of the lake's impact paired with the power of northeastern weather and the dramatic changes that come with the seasons. High waves crash against these clay spires when the gales of December through March turn their attention southward, stealing away the surfaces of these finlike spires and suffering only the most stubborn granules to remain.

Not so long ago, visitors could walk out along the tops of the chimneys—but those days have passed with the winter storms. Hikers are now confined to a narrow cliff edge from which we gain spectacular views of Chimney Bluffs and Lake Ontario's expanse. Deceptively calm from this height of 360 feet above lake level, the lake glistens serenely beneath the summer sunset, belying the tempest that created the rosy spires before you. The far horizon looks strangely solid, but the northern shore in Canada is 53 miles distant—too far to see, even from this height.

The trail leads down a shrub-lined path into a conifer forest, where low spots can be discouragingly muddy even in late spring. As the path emerges from the woods at the edge of the bluff, the Chimneys come into view. Watch out for the cliff edge—there's no railing here or anywhere along the Bluff Trail. Turn left to continue the loop along the cliff (there's a stairway down to another parking area to the right, if you've suddenly discovered a fear of ledges), which descends very gradually to the shoreline. The pebble beach at the end of the Bluff Trail may not look inviting at first glance, but it's a great place to stand to view the Chimney Bluffs from lake level as sunset turns them russet and golden.

Miles and Directions

0.0 Start at the parking lot and walk up the paved path until you see a mowed swath through the grasses to your right. Turn down this path and begin to cross the field of shrubs. You're on the park's East-West Trail.

0.6 Two trails converge here: The East-West Trail continues straight, while the Drumlin Trail goes left and right. Turn left onto the Drumlin Trail. Begin to pass through a conifer forest, with thick grapevines hanging from many of the trees.

1.1 Emerge from the woods at the Bluff Overlook. The Chimneys are to your left. Turn left and continue on the Bluff Trail. As you walk you'll notice that some parts of the trail have crumbled with erosion. In most cases visitors have worn new paths as alternatives to those that have fallen away. Watch your step on this trail, and stop walking when you want to admire the scenery.

1.7 A trail leads left, back into the woods. This is one of several connecting trails that take you back to the developed areas of the park and the parking lot. Turn left here to shorten your hike, or continue straight for more of the Bluff Trail.

1.9 When you come out of the woods, you're at lake level at a pebble beach. (FYI: You may want to stop here to stand on the beach and look back at the bluffs before departing.) Turn left and walk across the mowed grass to the paved path that leads to the parking area.

2.2 Arrive back at the parking lot and your vehicle.

14 Labrador Hollow State Unique Area

Stroll the boardwalk for a triple delight: forest-covered hills, bird-filled wetlands, and a sparkling glacial kettle pond.

Distance: 0.5-mile loop
Approximate hiking time: 30 minutes
Difficulty: Easy
Trail surface: Sturdy boardwalk
Best season: Year-round
Other trail users: None
Canine compatibility: Leashed dogs permitted
Fees and permits: No fees or permits required
Schedule: Open daily, dawn to dusk

Maps: Trail maps available online at www.cnyhiking.com/LabradorHollowUniqueArea.htm
Water availability: None
Trail contact: New York State Department of Environmental Conservation, Region 7 Division of Lands and Forests, 1285 Fisher Ave., Cortland, NY 13045; 607-753-3095; www.dec.ny.gov/outdoor/7792.html

Finding the trailhead: From Syracuse take I-81 South about 18 miles to Tully (exit 14). From Tully take NY 80 East 9.8 miles to NY 91 South. Watch for the sign on the right side of NY 91 for Labrador Hollow and the parking area. The boardwalk begins at the parking area. GPS: N42 47.560' / W76 03.143'

The Hike

How does a natural space qualify for the title of Unique Area? Not surprisingly, the qualifications are different for each property—that, after all, is what makes them unique. In the case of Labrador Hollow, the confluence of several kinds of topography—a narrow, glacially carved valley; surrounding hills several hundred feet high; a pine and hemlock swamp; and marshlands that provide a graceful transition to the open water of a glacial kettle pond—make this area unusually special. The Department of Environmental Conservation has made it easy for us to enjoy Labrador Hollow's scenic riches with the installation of a beautiful boardwalk system that brings visitors directly to quality viewpoints.

The 0.5-mile boardwalk leads through several different ecological zones, and the astute observer will see and hear the clues that separate one habitat from another. Wood thrushes and house wrens call in the wooded areas on dry land, while common yellowthroat and willow flycatcher songs dominate the wetlands. Spring peeper calls echo in the marshes, while the rubber-band call of the green frog becomes clearer as the boardwalk approaches the pond. Fiddlehead ferns and pink trilliums gain footholds in the drier area at the beginning of the walk, giving way in the wetland to lily pads and periphyton—a moisture-holding algae that delivers nutrition to plants in dry seasons.

Your walk may be brief, but you'll find plenty to see and hear in this singular environment.

Miles and Directions

0.0 Start at the parking area. Turn right as the loop begins. Pass through woods of mixed evergreens and leafy trees, where trillium and mayapple bloom in spring. Look out from the boardwalk to see the forested hills that define this valley—a stunning sight in autumn.

0.2 A built-in bench provides a great place to stop and admire the view of the hills. Continue around the loop and pass into a swampier area with fewer trees. Don't miss the dead, hollowed tree to your left, with its crazy assortment of woodpecker holes.

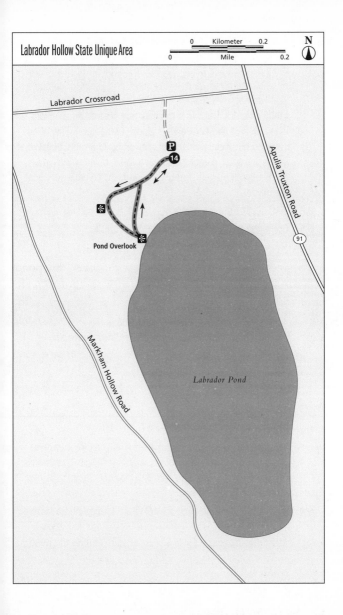

Labrador Hollow State Unique Area

Labrador Crossroad

Apulia Truxton Road

91

14

Pond Overlook

Markham Hollow Road

Labrador Pond

0.3 An area with open water appears to your right. Lily pads cover part of the pond, but you might still glimpse a swimming muskrat just below the surface. Look for ducks, geese, herons, and other water-loving birds, and listen for common yellowthroat, marsh wren, song and swamp sparrows, and many different frogs. In a moment you'll reach an excellent overlook for Labrador Pond, a glacial kettle pond. This pond came to be when a calving glacier dropped a huge block of ice in this spot, creating a cavity that filled with water when the ice block melted. Today this pond is a favorite with local canoeists.

0.4 Turn right at the intersection to return to the parking area.

0.5 Complete the loop and return to your vehicle.

15 Highland Forest County Park

Here's a forest sampler: A 2-mile loop through hardwood and evergreen woodlands to discover one of the area's most popular wilderness parklands.

Distance: 2.2-mile loop
Approximate hiking time: 1.25 hours
Difficulty: Moderate
Trail surface: Dirt path
Best season: Year-round
Other trail users: None on hiking trails; different trails for cyclists and skiers
Canine compatibility: Leashed dogs permitted on hiking trails only
Fees and permits: No fees or permits required
Schedule: Open daily at 8:30

a.m.; closing times: 4:30 p.m. Dec through Feb, 5:30 p.m. Mar and Nov, 6:30 p.m. Apr and Oct, 7:30 p.m. May and Sept, 8:30 p.m. June through Aug
Maps: Park map available online at onondagacountyparks.com/highland/
Water availability: At Skyline Lodge and at restrooms near Kernen Shelter
Trail contact: Onondaga County Parks, 106 Lake Dr., Liverpool 13088; (315) 451-7275; www.onondagacountyparks.com

Finding the trailhead: From Syracuse take I-81 South about 18 miles to Tully (exit 14). Drive 11 miles east on NY 80 to Highland Park Road and the entrance to the park. The trails begin at Skyland Lodge. GPS: N42 50.244' / W75 55.385'

The Hike

The oldest and most established of Onondaga County's parks, Highland Forest could serve as a model for parks on the national level. Its scrupulous organization of separate trails for foot traffic and bikes or skis, its clear trail markings that leave no room for confusion, and its meticulous maintenance of the trails all make this a world-class park. It's no wonder that everyone we consulted in the Syracuse area recommended that we include Highland Forest in this guide.

Trails in this park range from 0.5-mile wanders to a loop of nearly 9 miles. The North County National Scenic Trail—piggybacking here on the Onondaga Trail of the Finger Lakes Trail System—passes through the park as well. The shorter loop we've chosen allows you to get a sense of what this forest is about on a relatively easy trek, perhaps enticing you to make a longer trip on your next visit.

Begin at the Skyline Lodge by registering in the book at the front desk. With a park of this size—2,759 acres—it's important to let park management know where you're planning to be, so list the trails you plan to hike (Kernen Junction, Nature, and Limestone Trails) in the space provided. Pick up the brochure for the self-guided Nature Trail, which describes the stops in detail.

If you're hiking or cross-country skiing here in winter, the lodge offers breakfast and a selection of soups and sandwiches, all catered by Orchard Vali Restaurant of Lafayette in a dining room with a magnificent view. You can rent snowshoes here as well.

Over the creek and through the woods—you'll be glad you spent a day hiking in this wonderfully natural, unusually user-friendly park.

Miles and Directions

0.0 Start at Skyline Lodge and proceed to the well-marked trail gateway signs. Take the trail marked hiking/snowshoeing, and follow the maroon signs for the Kernen Junction Trail.

0.2 Turn left at the trail junction, following the Kernen Junction Trail.

0.3 Cross a dirt road and continue straight. The Finger Lakes and North Country National Scenic Trails join the trail here.

0.5 Turn right onto the Kernen Junction and Crossover Trails. (The Limestone and Crossover Trails also go straight here.) Cross the road ahead and continue straight.

0.6 The Kernen Shelter is to the right, and a parking lot appears on your left. There are restrooms here. Continue to the trailhead for the Nature Trail (green signs), where you see a wooden board with a clock, thermometer, and trail map. Begin the Nature Trail by walking down five steps to a bridge over the creek.

0.8 Cross two bridges over small streams.

0.9 Reach a junction at a larger bridge. The bike trails go left. Go right over the bridge, briefly sharing the trail with the bicycle/skiing routes. As you step off the bridge, turn immediately left to continue on the Nature Trail. Enter a particularly lovely evergreen forest in which the trees continue to grow at the top while they lose needles and branches below.

1.0 Cross another bridge and turn left at the trail junction. You are leaving the Crossover Trail (gold signs) and the Main Trail (orange signs) and walking exclusively on the Nature Trail.

1.1 Cross the bike trails and continue straight. At the turn go left on the Nature Trail.

1.3 Turn left onto the wide path toward the park office. Bear right ahead as you approach Torbert Shelter. Cross the parking lot to the left and pick up the trail at the information center kiosk on the southeast end of the parking lot, directly to your left. Turn right at the board with the clock and thermometer (do not take the Nature Trail). Follow the Kernen Junction Trail across the road.

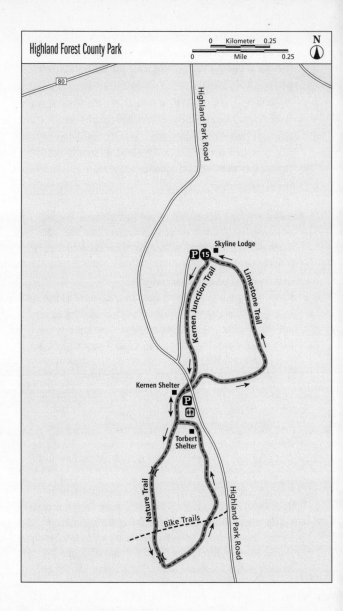

Highland Forest County Park

Skyline Lodge

Kernen Junction Trail

Limestone Trail

Kernen Shelter

Torbert Shelter

Nature Trail

Bike Trails

Highland Park Road

Highland Park Road

80

0   Kilometer   0.25

0   Mile   0.25

N

1.7 You've retraced your steps along the connecting portion of the Kernen Junction Trail; now bear right onto the Limestone Trail (pink signs). Cross a mowed area to the hiking/snow-shoeing trail sign. Pass under the sign and begin the Limestone Trail.

1.8 Cross the North County National Scenic Trail and continue straight. At the junction with the Main and Crossover Trails, turn left (the other trails go straight). Cross a wooden bridge over a wet area.

1.9 The Finger Lakes Trail goes left here. Continuing straight, cross another bridge over a wet spot and then a bridge over a small stream.

2.0 Walk up a set of steps defined by logs.

2.2 Emerge from the woods in the mowed yard of Skyline Lodge. Stop at the lodge to record your trail completion time in the register before returning to your vehicle.

16 Bear Swamp State Forest/Bird Conservation Area

You can lose the blues in this sun–dappled woodland, but you won't get lost on these well-marked trails through marshy bottomland and drier hardwood forest.

Distance: 3.0-mile loop
Approximate hiking time: 1.5 hours
Difficulty: Moderate
Trail surface: Dirt path
Best season: Year-round
Other trail users: Cross-country skiers, snowmobilers, trail runners, horseback riders
Canine compatibility: Leashed dogs permitted
Fees and permits: No fees or permits required

Schedule: Open daily, dawn to dusk
Maps: National Geographic Topo! New York/New Jersey edition
Water availability: None
Trail contact: New York State Department of Environmental Conservation, Region 7 Lands and Forests, 1285 Fisher Ave., Cortland, NY 13045; (607) 753-3095; www.dec.ny.gov/outdoor/7792.html

Finding the trailhead: From Syracuse take I-81 South about 22 miles to NY 281 (exit 13). Turn right onto NY 281 and continue 4.4 miles to Cold Brook Road; turn right. Drive to Long Road and turn left. Continue as Long Road becomes Glen Haven Road and then Grinnell Road. Turn right onto West Scott Road and continue 1.3 miles to Bear Swamp Road; keep right on Bear Swamp Road. In 2.1 miles turn left onto Hartnett Road. Park along the roadside near the trailhead for Trail 1. Look for a wooden display sign with a narrow trail running into the woods. GPS: N42 44.929' / W76 18.980'

The Hike

Now listed as a Bird Conservation Area as well as a state forest—in particular because of its nesting red-shouldered hawks, a species of special concern in New York State—Bear Swamp is a testament to reforestation as a viable way to reclaim clear-cut fields and turn them back into lush woodland. It's hard to imagine today that these 3,316 acres were used as farmland as recently as the 1930s, before the Great Depression drove many farmers to seek more lucrative employment.

When the farmers abandoned this land, New York State bought it up quickly, working with the Civilian Conservation Corps to plant Norway spruce, red and white pine, and larch. Other hardwoods were planted or migrated here on their own, especially the maple trees that cover so much northeastern land. In fall this forest fills with fiery shades of ruby, topaz, and gold when the leafy trees celebrate the change of seasons.

While its trails were constructed with cross-country skiing in mind, Bear Swamp offers an equally high-quality experience in spring, summer, and fall for hikers who can enjoy the well-established, clearly marked trails. Thirteen miles of trails provide many choices for hikers. We've chosen a loop that provides fairly easy walking through areas of managed forest and young hardwoods, moving from groves of pine and spruce to ash, cherry, and maple. This is a healthy forest enjoying responsible management, making this trail particularly appealing at any time of year.

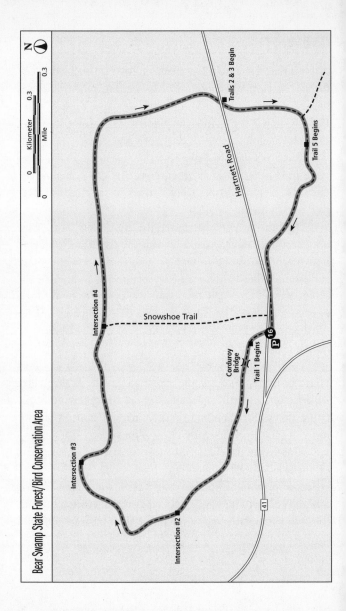

Bear Swamp State Forest/Bird Conservation Area

Miles and Directions

0.0 From Hartnett Road, you will see two paths: a wide path with a kiosk that bears a marker that says CY 44 and a narrow path to the left with a round orange marker that says TRAIL 1 in white print. Take the narrower path with the Trail 1 marker (the wider trail is for snowmobiles). In spring note the mounds of vinca (periwinkle) blooming at the trailhead. Trail 1 goes straight and to the left; turn left.

0.2 Cross a gravel-covered corduroy bridge over a small stream.

0.4 A drainage pipe forms a bridge over a small, slowly moving stream. Continue straight.

0.6 Come to a brown sign with a yellow "2" on it. This is Guidepost 2, part of the orientation system installed by the DEC. You've reached an old fire road, left over from the 1930s when fire lanes helped provide access to young conifer plantations. The surrounding red oak and red pine were planted during that time. Continue straight ahead.

0.8 At the intersection turn right and follow the Trail 1 signs.

1.0 Reach Guidepost 3. Turn right and continue to follow Trail 1. As you walk you may notice the difference between the forests on your right and left. The forest on your right has been thinned to allow new, young trees to germinate; the left-hand forest remains in its natural state.

1.4 At Guidepost 4 the snowmobile trail to the right leads back to Hartnett Road. (Option: If you'd like a quick way back to your car at this point, this is an easy exit route.) Continue straight.

2.1 A gravel and stone bridge crosses a little stream.

2.2 Come to Hartnett Road. From here the hike is a little more difficult, with some hilly terrain. (Option: To end your hike here, turn right and walk up the road to your car.) Cross the road and reenter the woods a little to the right, where you see an orange marker for Trail 4. Again, the ground around the entrance to the trail is covered in vinca.

2.3 A spur trail goes to the right. Continue left.

2.4 Cross a culvert over a stream and begin a steady incline to a barrier made of five large boulders, placed to keep motorized vehicles off the trail. Continue straight. A trail goes off to the left; pass it and take the next right.

2.5 A road goes left and right here. Cross and continue straight. At this point you're following the markers for Trail 5.

2.6 Here the trail goes left and right. Turn right and start down the hill. In a moment turn left to continue on Trail 5.

2.8 Take the trail to the left. Hartnett Road is now straight ahead.

2.9 Reach Hartnett Road again. Turn left and walk on the road to return to your car.

3.0 Complete the loop at your vehicle.

17 High Vista Preserve

A forest floor covered with wildflowers in late spring and summer, a small creek tributary meandering through a young forest . . . this peaceful woodland is a well-kept secret.

Distance: 1.8-mile lollipop
Approximate hiking time: 45 minutes
Difficulty: Easy
Trail surface: Dirt path
Best season: Apr through Nov
Other trail users: Hikers only
Canine compatibility: Leashed dogs permitted
Fees and permits: No fees or permits required
Schedule: Open daily, dawn to dusk, Apr through Nov; road to preserve not plowed Dec 1

to Apr 1
Maps: Finger Lakes Land Trust; map available online at www .fllt.org
Water availability: None
Trail contact: Finger Lakes Land Trust, 202 East Court St., Ithaca 14850; (607) 275-9487; www .fllt.org
Special considerations: Creek crossings may be difficult in early spring and after heavy rain (no bridges).

Finding the trailhead: From NY 41 south of Skaneateles, turn onto Vincent Hill Road West, just north of the Cortland/Onondaga County line. Drive about 0.3 mile to a small parking area on the right side of the road. The trail begins across the road, about 0.2 mile from the parking area. GPS: N42 46.230' / W76 15.655'

The Hike

Once upon a time, these 120 acres lay open and denuded on this sunny hillside, but those days are long gone. And while this little preserve retains the word "vista" in its name, the only view here peers deeper into the fairly young woods that now cover the terrain. The Finger Lakes Land Trust acquired this property back in 1993, and the organization now maintains the trail and looks after the woods, wetland, and ravine that grace the land.

The simple loop hike wanders first through an old orchard, followed by young hardwoods and hemlocks. The trail crosses a number of small streams and the larger Fair Haven Creek and wanders past clusters of wildflowers in spring, from violets and trillium to wild strawberry and jack-in-the-pulpit. Many fern species fill the gaps between wild-flowers, creating a sheltering understory for ground-feeding birds, chipmunks, squirrels, and other small animals.

The real treat here is the opportunity to spot cerulean warblers, which nest in the preserve, and many other war-blers from late April through May. As in any hardwood forest, woodpeckers can be heard hammering in the trees—watch for northern flicker and downy, hairy, and red-bellied woodpeckers.

As for that high vista . . . if you hike here in late fall or early spring, when the trees are without leaves, you can glimpse the southern end of Skaneateles Lake from the highest points on the trail.

Miles and Directions

0.0 Start from the parking area and walk up the road to the trail-head.

0.2 The trail begins here to your left; enter the preserve and fol-low the blue blazes.

0.5 The intersection is the beginning of the loop. Take the left branch.

0.7 Cross Fair Haven Creek on big, flat rocks. This may be tricky in spring when the creek rises with snowmelt.

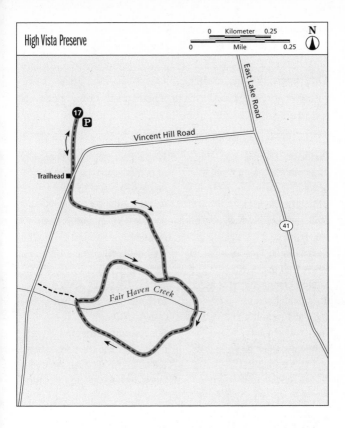

High Vista Preserve

0 Kilometer 0.25
0 Mile 0.25
N

East Lake Road

17 P

Vincent Hill Road

Trailhead ■

41

Fair Haven Creek

1.0 Reach the junction with the yellow trail to the left. (This trail leads out to Vincent Hill Road.) Bear right on the blue trail.

1.1 Cross Fair Haven Creek again. You may need to hunt for the best place to cross, particularly in spring. There are several spots with large rocks that are close enough together to provide solid footing.

1.3 Complete the loop. Turn left and follow the trail back out to your vehicle.

1.8 Arrive back at the parking area.

18 Fillmore Glen State Park

One waterfall after another tumbles through a narrow, lushly forested gorge, making this a delicious hike on a hot summer day.

Distance: 2.4-mile loop
Approximate hiking time: 1.5 hours
Difficulty: Moderate
Trail surface: Dirt path, some stone stairs
Best season: June through Oct
Other trail users: None
Canine compatibility: Leashed dogs permitted
Fees and permits: Entry fee per vehicle in season
Schedule: Open dawn to dusk, mid-May to mid-Oct

Maps: Park map available online at nysparks.state.ny.us/parks/info.asp?parkID=35
Water availability: Restrooms at main pavilion and in campground
Trail contact: Fillmore Glen State Park, 1686 SR 38, Moravia 13118; (315) 497-0139; nysparks.state.ny.us/parks/info.asp?parkID=35
Special considerations: If visiting in May, call the park to check the trail opening date. Watch for fallen, loose shale on the path.

Finding the trailhead: From Syracuse take NY 5 West about 22 miles to the junction with NY 38 in Auburn. Turn south onto NY 38 and continue 17 miles to the park entrance in Moravia. Park at the main pavilion; the trailhead is behind the building and up the paved path. GPS: N42 41.932' / W76 24.981'

The Hike

If you're only going to take one hike recommended in this guide, make it Fillmore Glen. Rarely do we find such a magical combination of striking geological formations, glistening gorge walls that weep with spring runoff, a storybook forest, and no fewer than five waterfalls—including one that plummets from a creek tributary at the top of the gorge. Tie all of this with an ingenious system of eight bridges that cross and recross the gorge, laced together by a pathway reinforced with natural stone guard walls, and you have the kind of hiking experience for which the Finger Lakes region is famous.

It's no surprise that glaciers played the initial role in shaping the gorge as the rush of glacial meltwater tore through the area and slashed through the surface shale to the limestone bedrock below. Today the surrounding shale continues to erode—you're likely to see recent crumbles as you hike—but the tenacious vegetation plays a role in holding much of it in place, covering the jagged rock faces with mosses, lichens, and vines.

While this hike is fairly easy in dry weather, the gorge creates a microclimate in which the humidity remains high. Stone steps and earthen pathways can be slippery, and water often drips (or cascades) from the porous shale walls, especially after a heavy rain. Two words to the wise on this:

(1) Wear footwear that will grip in wet situations.

(2) Don't miss the hanging gardens of ferns and clinging vines that result from the constant seeps through the multilayered shale.

Chances are, you don't often think about the thirteenth president of the United States, so it may not occur to you that this park is actually named for him. Millard Fillmore was born in this area, just outside Moravia, and the park contains a replica of the cabin in which he was born. You'll find it as you proceed to the main pavilion to begin your hike; it's on the south side of the parking area.

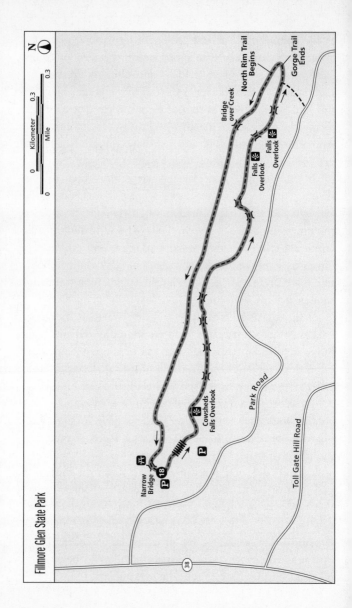

Fillmore Glen State Park

N

0   0.3
Kilometer
0   0.3
Mile

Narrow
Bridge

Cowsheds
Falls Overlook

Bridge
over Creek

North Rim Trail
Begins

Gorge Trail
Ends

Falls
Overlook

Falls
Overlook

Park Road

Toll Gate Hill Road

38

Miles and Directions

0.0 Start at the trailhead behind the pavilion and up the paved path.

0.1 The swimming area is to the left of the path, created by one of two dams in Dry Creek. Keep right and continue on the paved path.

0.2 Turn right onto the Gorge Trail. (Don't cross the bridge here; that's the route to the North Rim.) Take the stairway to the right; it's 140 steps to the top. (Option: Park in the lot at the top of the stairs to save yourself the fairly aerobic climb.) At the top of the steps turn left on the Gorge Trail.

0.3 Reach the overlook for Cowsheds Falls. Turn right and continue to the first of eight bridges.

0.4 Cross Bridge 1 and enter the dense, sultry forest. Stop here a moment to notice the fascinating patterns of moss on the trees and the change in the light quality as the sun works to filter through the leafy canopy. On the other side of this patch of forest, cross Bridge 2.

0.5 Cross Bridge 3.

0.6 Cross Bridge 4 and begin a steady incline.

0.7 Reach the top of the incline and a small waterfall.

0.8 Cross a series of platforms over runoff streams.

0.9 Cross Bridges 5 and 6.

1.0 A tributary creek originating at the top of the gorge sends a spectacular waterfall down through the glen wall. As you continue on the trail, don't miss the hanging gardens created by the seeps through the stacked shale walls.

1.1 Cross Bridge 7 and go up a staircase of about thirty steps.

1.2 Walk down sixteen steps to a falls overlook. When you're ready, walk up sixteen steps on the other side of the overlook and continue on the trail.

1.3 Come to Bridge 8, the last bridge on the Gorge Trail. The South Rim Trail crosses the bridge. To complete the Gorge

Trail, do not cross this bridge—continue straight. To follow the North Rim Trail to make a loop, as described here, continue straight as well. In about 200 feet the Gorge Trail ends. (Option: Return to the trailhead by retracing your steps on the Gorge Trail.) To continue the loop, climb to the North Rim using the switchbacks ahead. (FYI: The climb to the North Rim involves a 150-foot elevation change.)

1.4 At the top of the gorge turn left on the North Rim Trail. Cross a little bridge over a feeder stream.

1.7 Reach the source of the large waterfall you saw in the gorge. Cross a bridge over this tributary creek.

2.3 After a gentle descent on stone steps, bear left on the fork in the trail and proceed down a series of steps defined by railroad ties, followed by more stone steps. At the bottom you've reached Dry Creek and the picnic area on the north side of the gorge. Bear right and cross the parking lot to your left.

2.4 Cross the creek using the narrow bridge over the spillway, and arrive back at your vehicle in the parking lot.

Clubs and Trail Groups

- Adirondack Mountain Club, Onondaga Chapter; www.adk-on.org. The club offers a variety of hikes and programs to share the joy and knowledge of outdoor recreation.

- Syracuse Area Outdoor Adventure Club; www.meetup.com/adventurers-103/. For people who want to get outside, have fun, and meet others with similar interests, the group holds regularly scheduled hikes and seasonal adventures.

- Onondaga Audubon Society, P.O. Box 620, Syracuse 13201; www.onondagaaudubon.org. Onondaga Audubon promotes a greater appreciation of wildlife, land, water, and other natural resources through field trips, sanctuary management, and environmental education.

- Syracuse University Outing Club; suoc.syr.edu/. Students of Syracuse University and the SUNY College of Environmental Science and Forestry join to promote the enjoyment of the national environment with many trips and outings.

- Finger Lakes Land Trust, 202 East Court St., Ithaca 14850; (607) 275-9487; www.fllt.org. This nonprofit land trust works to preserve lands that define the character of the Finger Lakes region.

Day Hiker Checklist

- ❏ camera/film
- ❏ compass/GPS unit
- ❏ pedometer
- ❏ daypack
- ❏ first-aid kit
- ❏ food
- ❏ guidebook
- ❏ headlamp/flashlight with extra batteries and bulbs
- ❏ hat
- ❏ insect repellent
- ❏ knife/multipurpose tool
- ❏ map
- ❏ matches in waterproof container and fire starter
- ❏ fleece jacket
- ❏ rain gear
- ❏ sunglasses
- ❏ sunscreen
- ❏ swimsuit
- ❏ watch
- ❏ water
- ❏ water bottles/water hydration system

About the Author

Randi Minetor has written twenty-three books to date for the Globe Pequot Press (GPP), including the Passport to Your National Parks® Companion Guides series and National Park Pocket Guides for the Great Smoky Mountains, Zion and Bryce Canyon, Acadia, and Everglades National Parks and Gulf Islands National Seashore. Her other GPP books include five in the Timeline series: Gettysburg; Washington, D.C.; Fredericksburg; New York Immigrant Experience; and New Orleans.

Her husband, Nic Minetor, is the photographer for her Pocket Guides and Timeline Tours books, and they have hiked in upstate New York for three other guides in the Best Easy Day Hikes series covering Rochester, Buffalo, and Albany, New York. Randi is also the national parks Examiner on Examiner.com. She and Nic live in Rochester.

What's So Special about Unspoiled, Natural Places?

Beauty   Solitude   Wildness   Freedom   Quiet   Adventure
Serenity   Inspiration   Wonder   Excitement
Relaxation   Challenge

There's a lot to love about our treasured public lands, and the reasons are different for each of us. Whatever your reasons are, the national **Leave No Trace** education program will help you discover special outdoor places, enjoy them, and preserve them—today and for those who follow. By practicing and passing along these simple principles, you can help protect the special places you love from being loved to death.

The Principles of **Leave No Trace**

- Plan ahead and prepare
- Travel and camp on durable surfaces
- Dispose of waste properly
- Leave what you find
- Minimize campfire impacts
- Respect wildlife
- Be considerate of other visitors

Leave No Trace is a national nonprofit organization dedicated to teaching responsible outdoor recreation skills and ethics to everyone who enjoys spending time outdoors.

To learn more or to become a member, please visit us at www.LNT.org or call (800) 332–4100.

Leave No Trace, P.O. Box 997, Boulder, CO 80306